D0406879

FLOWERING TREES

Flowering Trees

by

Robert B. Clark

Drawings by D A R R E L L   S W E E T

D. Van Nostrand Company, Inc.
Princeton, New Jersey
Toronto • New York • London

D. VAN NOSTRAND COMPANY, INC.
120 Alexander St., Princeton, New Jersey (*Principal office*)
24 West 40 Street, New York 18, New York

D. VAN NOSTRAND COMPANY, LTD.
358, Kensington High Street, London, W.14, England

D. VAN NOSTRAND COMPANY (Canada), LTD.
25 Hollinger Road, Toronto 16, Canada

COPYRIGHT © 1963, BY
D. VAN NOSTRAND COMPANY, INC.

Published simultaneously in Canada by
D. VAN NOSTRAND COMPANY (Canada), LTD.

No reproduction in any form of this book, in whole or in part (except for brief quotation in critical articles or reviews), may be made without written authorization from the publishers.

To
LYLE L. BLUNDELL

Emeritus Professor of Landscape Architecture
University of Massachusetts

KEEN PLANTSMAN, DEDICATED TEACHER
AND INSPIRING FRIEND

THIS VOLUME IS AFFECTIONATELY INSCRIBED

Preface

Over the years I have grown flowering trees, written about them and recommended them to many hundreds of home owners, with invariably excellent results. Dogwoods, crabapples, cherries, magnolias, and other flowering trees are versatile and have many assets besides flowers—fruit, foliage, and other characteristics that give them a year-round appeal.

The book's purpose is to familiarize you with the small-to-moderate-height deciduous trees that bloom superbly in the northern cold-winter regions of the country. Of course, many of these trees also bloom with equal (sometimes greater) distinction in milder regions. But, with a few exceptions, I have omitted the forest-size shade trees and the strictly tropical or subtropical species, or merely cited them, for they are subjects in themselves.

Although *all* trees bear flowers, there are a number of ornamental small trees whose floral displays are usually inconspicuous. This is also true of most of the tall-growing shade trees. Such trees are frequently mentioned in the vaious chapters but I have concentrated on trees—and certain treelike shrubs—whose blossoming is regarded by all as a major attribute. (The principal difference between trees and shrubs is that trees renew themselves each year at the tips of the branches whereas shrubs in most cases send up new canes from the ground.)

Throughout the book I have referred to trees by common name wherever possible, with scientific names following. The scientific names accord with the international codes of botanical and horticultural nomenclature; the manuals I used for guidance in nomenclature were Bailey's *Hortus Second,* Blackburn's *Trees and Shrubs in Eastern North America,* and Rehder's *Manual of Cultivated Trees and Shrubs.*

This book is the fruit of the knowledge and generosity of many patient and talented individuals. I wish herewith to acknowledge my great indebtedness to them. I offer deep gratitude to: the several directors of the Arnold Arboretum, the Missouri Botanical Garden and the New Jersey Agricultural Experiment Station who graciously made available the facilities of their institutions for study and their staffs for consultation; to Mr. Darrell Sweet, whose superb illustrations provide the basis upon which the text is mere commentary; to Benjamin Blackburn, David Fales, Arthur Harmount Graves, and Charles G. Osgood, whose timely suggestions were invaluable; to Miss Beverly M. Buker, Mrs. Ernest G. Christ and Mrs. Theodore Strawinski, for preparation of my original manuscript, and to several friends whose sustained interest in this project has witnessed its blooming. Finally for whatever blemishes occur I assume complete responsibility.

Contents

		PAGE
	Preface	vii
1.	FLOWERING TREES—USEFUL BEAUTY	1
2.	SELECTING AND PLACING YOUR FLOWERING TREES	5
3.	FRUIT, FRAGRANCE, FORM, AND FOLIAGE	10
4.	HANDSOME HORIZONTALS IN DOGWOODS	27
5.	CRABAPPLES MEAN LANDSCAPE LOVELINESS	38
6.	MAGNOLIAS FOR MAGNIFICENCE	48
7.	CHERRIES FOR MISTS OF WHITE AND PINK	59
8.	FLOWERING TREES GALORE—A GUIDE TO FORTY-ODD MORE	73
9.	POSSIBLE PROBLEMS	141
10.	GROW YOUR OWN FLOWERING TREES	155
11.	TRANSPLANTING	165
12.	MAINTENANCE PRUNING	171
	Appendices	
I.	TREE TRAITS	174
II.	SPECIAL USES FOR FLOWERING TREES	186
III.	SEQUENCE OF BLOOM	194
IV.	FLOWER IDENTIFICATION	196
V.	FLOWERING TREES WITH FLESHY FRUITS	204
VI.	AUTUMN FOLIAGE COLORS	207
VII.	FORCING BRANCHES	209
VIII.	WHERE TO SEE FLOWERING TREES	212
IX.	TREE TERMS TO KNOW	222
	INDEX	235

List of Illustrations

IN COLOR

FACING PAGE

I.	Japanese Flowering Crabapple	20
II.	Purple Lennei Magnolia	52
III.	Weeping Higan Cherry	84
IV.	Ruby Horse-chestnut	116
V.	Waterer's Golden-chain	148
VI.	Tulip-tree	180

IN BLACK AND WHITE

PAGE

1.	Empress-tree, pods	13
2.	Empress-tree, buds	25
3.	Dogwood, flowering branch	28
4.	Cornelian-cherry, buds	34
5.	Star Magnolia, flowering branch	50
6.	Star Magnolia, flower and pod	51
7.	Kobus Magnolia, flowering branch	53
8.	Saucer Magnolia, flower and pod	54
9.	Lennei Magnolia, flowering branch	55
10.	Gray Birch, catkin	79
11.	Chestnut, flowering branch	83
12.	Epaulette-tree, flowering branch	90
13.	Epaulette-tree, fruits	91
14.	Goldenrain-tree, flowering branch	96
15.	Hawthorn, flowering branch	98
16.	Linden, flowering branch	102
17.	Callery Pear, flowering branch	108

LIST OF ILLUSTRATIONS

		PAGE
18.	Redbud, flowering branch	112
19.	Chinese Scholar-tree, fruits	115
20.	Service-berry, flowering branch	117
21.	Silverbell, flowering branch	120
22.	Silverbell, fruits	121
23.	Smoke-tree, fruits	123
24.	Snowbell, fruits	126
25.	Stewartia, flowering branch	129
26.	Tree of Heaven, fruits	131
27.	Tulip-tree, pods	135
28.	Black-haw, buds	138

1

Flowering Trees—
Useful Beauty

The foremost asset of flowering trees, of course, is their great floral beauty, predominantly in shades of white, yellow and pink. In most cases, and with favorable weather, each tree's display will last for weeks. The flowers of many trees are fragrant, ranging from a delicate sweetness to a rich perfume.

The majority of hardy flowering trees put on their show in spring. Several kinds bloom in summer, when their carefree floral bounty and the cooling effect of their foliage are doubly welcome. By planting a selection of long-blooming varieties—and with an assist from the weather—you can have a virtually continuous parade of blossoms from late winter or early spring through late summer or early fall.

FLOWERING TREES

The spring-flowering kinds give you a bonus: you can cut some of their branches in late winter and force them into bloom indoors in a vase of water for your own private preview of spring.

In addition to their notable seasonal bloom, flowering trees are distinctive in foliage for six to seven months or more—spanning three seasons. Being deciduous, the trees are bare of foliage in winter, but before the leaves drop, they exchange their natural green for a variety of eye-filling autumnal hues. This adds another gay color note to the home property, sometimes more striking than when the trees were in full bloom.

Flowering trees are appealing in or out of bloom. Many kinds produce fruit that is highly ornamental and often remains colorful throughout fall and winter. Some of these fruits are table delicacies; all are attractive to birds and squirrels.

Most of the trees also have notable branch structure, handsome or unusual bark, and intriguing buds, so they are decorative even when dormant and leafless in winter.

There are flowering trees of every form and size, from spreading or weeping to narrowly upright, and from ten feet high to fifty feet or more. From spring through autumn, all but the youngest, smallest trees will cast pleasant shade and "create" breezes—or act as a buffer

2

when the wind is strong. Since they are deciduous, they do not shade the house or terrace from the winter's weak but welcome sunlight. All of these characteristics combine to provide your property with natural air-conditioning or what might be called natural climate control.

LANDSCAPE ANCHOR

Flowering trees are wonderfully effective in "tying" a house to the surrounding land. They frame the house and give it an air of dignity and permanence. That last point is especially important to you if your home is in a treeless housing development. Of course, large trees have an immediate impact, but if your budget allows you to plant only saplings, most will still give you substantial effects in a very few years.

You will find that flowering trees make lovely garden pictures in combination with other landscape plants such as broadleaved and needled evergreen trees and shrubs, deciduous flowering shrubs, groundcovers, perennials and bulb plantings. Flowering trees can be used as height accents in a shrub border, or as fillers among tall trees.

Flowering trees are as easy to grow as other woody plants. There are kinds you can grow no matter what cultural conditions your property affords. You can find varieties adaptable to clay, sand, wet, dry, acid and alkaline soils. And there are sturdy species that can withstand the perils of sooty cities.

Even the smallest home property in the city or suburbs can accommodate one or two flowering trees of low stature, but many home owners are quite unaware of the possibilities open to them. Study some of the fine color-illustrated nursery catalogues, visit well-labeled plantings in local nurseries, parks, and botanical gardens, and look at neighborhood gardens. Such observation will help you select trees that suit your landscape requirements and conditions and that possess the finest flowers and the maximum number of beauty points over and above flowers.

2

Selecting and Placing Your Flowering Trees

Garden making gives us the pleasure of choosing. "Shall I have crabapples and azaleas, or had it better be dogwoods instead of crabapples? Would viburnums also fit into the composition?" The practical-minded gardener, however, will hinge most of his plant choices on one very practical consideration: the kinds of plants that can be expected to flourish in the available situation. He must know about cultural tolerances and requirements —the ability of various plants to grow under the limitations of the particular garden. As an extreme example, it would be futile to attempt to raise palm trees in northern gardens, rhododendrons in limestone soils, or cactus in boggy sites.

FLOWERING TREES

Consider the Setting

A main requirement for achieving an inviting garden is a proper setting. It is just as important to think of the setting when you display your beautiful flowering plants in the garden as it is when you decorate your home with flowers. The shy cardinal flower reflected in the cool dark waters of the mountain stream creates an unforgettable impression. The unobtrusive weight of August foliage and the peaceful sound of the trickling water combine to imprint beauty upon receptive senses.

Flowering trees challenge the imaginative gardener; he must strive to show them to best advantage. Trees in a grouping of many kinds must be skillfully placed so that the effect of one tree does not spoil the delight afforded by a neighboring one. If you wish to have a collection of different kinds of flowering trees, you will need a large area. A small garden had better be devoted to a few kinds or even one charmingly grown specimen. An individual weeping Higan cherry against a backdrop of spruce can glorify spring's arrival as joyously as a hillside of bright daffodils or forsythia.

SELECTING AND PLACING YOUR FLOWERING TREES

PLAN YOUR PLANTINGS

You can bring beauty into your garden, even in a small area, by observing a few simple rules. The successful garden is usually enclosed. It has a boundary which clearly defines the space within and makes it easier to visualize and execute a plan.

One possible plan would be a succession of bloom throughout the year. Another might be the harmonious blending of several kinds of plants into an exciting composition for a special season. Still a third scheme would be to devote the garden to a favorite family or group of flowering trees—those requiring acid soil, or tolerating soils that are poorly drained, or shade tolerant plants, or plants that attract wild life. The range of choice is bounded only by your imagination.

While you are making up your mind, do some actual shopping for particular specimens. Today's quality nursery stock can be purchased in a variety of ways: from mail order nurseries and local nurseries or garden centers and even landscape companies. Visits to nurseries or service garden centers are invaluable if you wish to see what is available and to judge each plant's beauty and suitability for your particular needs. In many instances you will see plants that have been grown directly in large metal cans or other containers so that their roots are conditioned for transplanting.

SIGNS TO BUY BY

In walking about the sales yard with its fragrant and cheerful flowering plants, your impulse may be to select those specimens with the largest number of blooms. Do not be too hasty however. Healthy and vigorous growth is a safer criterion of quality. Look for the type of growth the plant made last year. The branchlets should be sturdy and brightly colored. If the current year's foliage is mature, it should be an attractive green and full-bodied, not wilted, misshapen or blemished.

Roots? If the dealer is known to you, you should not have to worry. Be sure that the roots are firmly knit throughout the burlapped soil ball or in the container. They should not project through the burlap or container or they may be broken in transit or transplanting, and the plants may not survive.

In cash and carry sales, many nurserymen offer replacement on the basis of 50 percent of purchase price. They usually give suggestions on planting but this service is available also through your county agricultural agent's office. In any event, the nurseryman expects you to give the plant reasonable care. It was alive when it left his sales yard. If it was too large for easy handling and he arranged to plant it, and still it failed to survive transplanting within one year's time, he frequently will agree to replace it for the cost of labor involved to replant another tree.

An established nurseryman is proud of the stock he offers for sale. If price is a factor with you, then smaller-sized stock—not lower quality—should be considered. The tree size which, under best conditions, will produce bloom the following growing season is usually five to six feet, although other sizes may prove satisfactory.

3

Fruit, Fragrance, Form, and Foliage

While flowers are unquestionably the principal feature, they are not the only beauty mark of most flowering trees. Let us now explore in a general way the several other features—fruit, fragrance, foliage (including autumn leaf colors), tree form (branch patterns), bark, twigs and buds—that can give a tree much more than one-season appeal. These features are discussed in more specific detail under each tree's separate heading throughout the course of the book. Most of these extra assets are also cited for easy reference in the listings in the Appendices. The trees that possess these beauty marks in greatest abundance are, obviously, most worthy of your consideration, for you want to select the species that will be decorative not only during their flowering period but all through the year.

FRUIT

The fruit that follows flowers provides a second season of attraction from flowering trees. To be sure, not every species makes a conspicuous fruit display. Some do not ripen any fruit to speak of. However, most flowering trees bear seed cases, at least, that are useful in flower arrangements or even as foods. The seed-pod season extends throughout the summer well into winter. The outstanding fruit display of most northern-region flowering trees takes place in September-October as the foliage falls. Many fruits are colorful while ripening. The fruits are generally classed by the way they ripen—dry or fleshy.

Fleshy fruits, such as those of crabapples, cherries and dogwood berries, turn bright red or yellow when ripe. Often they are luscious, providing food for the table or for wildlife. They bring color and interest into the garden and refreshment to the gardener. Berried branches may be brought into the house for decoration.

The bird-feeding aspect is important. Besides being pleasant company, songbirds are an effective ally of the gardener in his battle with insect enemies. Birds are the best guardians of the garden during the gardener's mid-

11

summer absence. Numerous flowering trees provide forage for the birds.

On the calendar of fruit production, the first native fruits ripen in June on the service-berry. July provides cherries and plums while August sees the birds attracted to giant dogwood and Siebold viburnum. By September so many berried shrubs and trees have ripened fruits that migrating flocks have a wide choice of food. Unfortunately they sometimes ravenously strip the entire crop from individual trees in a day.

Colorful berried branches, used alone or with other material in arrangements, provide the note of fruitful abundance in autumn decoration. Feathered, wispy, fruiting stalks of the smoke-tree are available throughout the summer. In August, clusters of orange berries from mountain-ash become ripe. The clusters are made up of a dozen or more tiny apple-like berries arranged in a broad flat head. The foliage consists of small, oblong, fine-toothed leaflets. *Photinia villosa* has similar berries but they are red and fewer in number; the foliage is undivided. Russian-olive bears small silvered olivelike berries amid the silvery gray leaves.

If you are contemplating a home-grown feast, you must keep ahead of the birds and squirrels. These descend upon your favorite crop without notice and steal the

1. The Empress-tree's pointed, egg-shaped pods that split lengthwise are decorative in dried arrangements; pods contain tiny winged seeds in great numbers.

harvest practically under your eyes. But it is worth trying to save some of it, for nothing quite equals tree-ripened fruits. Cornelian-cherries that ripen in July make excellent jelly. August is the season of luscious peaches, while more plums and the crabapples arrive in September. Tart fruits make delectable jellies, and tree-ripened plums are excellent dessert fruits. Roasted chestnuts are choice autumn delicacies.

Dried fruits are decorative in winter arrangements. Do not let pods shatter or husks split, for then tiny seeds will spill over table and carpet. Dip these fruits in colorless plastic material, or spray them with plastic from an aerosol can to give them a clear coating that will prevent shattering in the dry indoor atmosphere.

Lindens, silverbells and tulip-tree have winged seeds. Pod fruits are borne by the legumes, including locust, redbud, silk-tree, yellowwood, golden-chain and maackia. Capsuled fruits, such as those of beebee and empress-trees, and lilac, sourwood, and white alder, are beautifully fashioned for dried bouquets.

Emphasizing Fragrance

Fragrance calls up distant places, happy events. No garden can afford to be without fragrance. Fortunately the number of flowering trees with scented blooms is large.

The sequence begins in early April with the magnolias.

Several magnolias emit scents that are sweet and pervading. Others produce heavy, musky perfumes. Two American species, the sweetbay and bullbay magnolias, suggest Southern hospitality. Most of the oriental magnolias are sweetly scented. The Oyama magnolia, *Magnolia Sieboldii*, a shrubby plant with nodding flowers, suggests the fragrance of the pink lady's slipper orchid. Crushed leaves of *Magnolia salicifolia* are reminiscent of anise.

Certain cherries provide fragrance, in addition to profusion of bloom. The single-flowered white Yoshino cherry has a faint scent, while some of the Japanese flowering cherries, which extend the cherry blossom season, carry a bonus of fragrance. Those possessing exceptional perfume are 'Jo-nioi,' Japanese for supreme fragrance, 'Sirotae,' sometimes called 'Mount Fuji,' and 'Amanogawa,' the Japanese term for the milky way. Paleness of bloom appears to be associated with scent. The popular deep pink variety 'Kwanzan' is virtually scentless.

Crabapples are well known for their delicate fragrance. Sweetest perhaps is the Siberian crabapple whose white, pendent, cup-shaped blooms perfume the spring air with an ambrosial fragrance. Apple orchards in blossom are

15

memorable not alone for color but equally for their subtle perfume. Among shade trees, the lindens (or basswood) are famous for floral fragrance.

Sweet-smelling white flowers are borne in clusters by the snowbell, black locust and yellowwood. The Washington hawthorn, which bears flat clusters at the tips of short shoots, furnishes nectar for bees but has an odor not especially attractive to man. Tulip-tree, Russian-olive and idesia produce copious amounts of nectar from yellow or greenish flowers. The tulip-tree, *(Liriodendron Tulipifera),* or yellow poplar, as it is called by the forester, has large single blooms at the tips of short shoots after the foliage has expanded. Honeybees are delighted by its profusion of bloom. Its flower does resemble a tulip, but only superficially in structure and certainly not in showiness. The greenish yellow petals with large brown spots are all but hidden among the leaves in late May.

The Russian-olive's tiny single blooms, sweetly scented and attractive to bees, are hidden among silvery gray leaves. Among the idesia's large two-toned leaves, greenish clusters of fragrant flowers may be discovered. These hang in huge grapelike clusters, the sexes separate on different trees.

There are more than thirty flowering trees having fragrant blooms. The season of fragrance extends from earliest spring to midsummer. Among these trees, various categories of height, shape and flower color (except red and red-purple) are represented. The selection is large among fragrant flowering trees.

FINE FOLIAGE

What a variety of green hues we have among tree leaves. Not only do the shades vary from plant to plant, but they also change from season to season. The late-season aspect is not the midsummer hue nor the springtime freshness; yet it is green. Each tree has its own coloring.

Color notes for relief of monochromatic greens may be introduced into the landscape composition, but gray-, red-, or blue-toned foliage need to be used with restraint. Plants with foliage that is not green are beautiful only when their position actually relieves monotony or adds zest and sparkle. Red in foliage is a dull color that produces the effect of weight. Bluish green and gray create the illusion of distance and space. At their best, plants with off-colored foliage afford striking contrasts and accents, but too many loud notes only produce clangor.

Another feature which might influence your choice is the compound leaves of certain flowering trees. The leaflets fall in segments and do not collect on the ground in heaps, so lawn maintenance is reduced. The legumes, including locust, scholar-tree and yellowwood, belong to this group. Beebee-tree and goldenrain also have compound leaves that do not create a nuisance when they fall.

Refined effects of shade and background can be obtained from such trees as black locust, scholar-tree and Russian-olive. The last-named has a narrow grayish leaf that makes the tree lovely when viewed from a distance. Bluish-green foliage of refined texture is well displayed by the black locust. In case you live by the ocean, both the Russian-olive and the black locust are adapted to seashore gardens.

Bold foliage masses are features of chestnuts, horse-chestnuts and idesia, and also of the dove-tree whose leaves unfold in early May as its huge white bracts are expanding; these heart-shaped leaves are coarse-toothed and dark green. The Siebold viburnum bears dark green oval-shaped leaves, three to six inches long, having a lustrous rough surface and coarse teeth. The oriental flowering cherry has egg-shaped leaves, two and one-half to five inches long, with a long tapering point and sharp teeth. Wart-like glands may be seen on either side of the leaf stalk near the base of the blade. The empress-tree and the fringe-tree expand their leaves after the flowers unfold. The leaves of the empress-tree are heart-shaped, five to ten inches long, and covered on both surfaces with velvety hairs. Those of the fringe-tree are elliptic and toothless, three to eight inches long.

Autumn Foliage Color

Brilliant and breath-taking are the hues of foliage in late September and early October. The Northeast is especially famous for spectacular fall foliage displays. When days become shorter and cold nights alternate with warm sunshiny days, when the nitrogen supply becomes depleted and rainfall is scant, then the leaves cease to manufacture sugars and starches and lose their green, as the tree begins to draw starch down into stems and roots. This is a brief explanation of the remarkable chemical transformation that creates the gorgeous display of foliage colors in fall.

Until this annual miracle occurs, green chlorophyll masks the basic yellows and reds in tree leaves. Carotin, the substance which gives carrots their familiar color, and xanthophyll, another pigment, are responsible for the yellows. Gray birch and tulip-tree are among the first native trees to become a glowing yellow in fall. The Chinese scholar-tree assumes stunning hues if the season

19

remains warm into November. Spectacular and subtle reds and purples owe their color to the pigment anthocyanin.

BRANCHES—TREE FORM

The scaffold pattern of a tree's branches varies according to the species. The crown development represents the growth history of the leading shoot and the adjustment of the side branches to it. Each twig grows toward the light. Lateral branches are at a disadvantage and are obliged to accommodate themselves to whatever space becomes available once the leader has assumed its position. Side shoot growth therefore will be less perfectly developed than the leaves and buds of the principal shoot.

Ideally, the shape that trees assume is the conical form of the Christmas tree with the primary shoot uppermost and the lateral ones disposed in whorls below and on the sides. Such a pattern is common during the youth of many types of trees. The tulip-tree is an excellent example. There comes a time with most plants, however, when the leading shoot no longer is able to maintain its annual pace of elongation, and the lateral ones approach or overtake it in rate of growth. The tree subsequently takes on

20

I. The Japanese Flowering Crabapple becomes picturesque as it ages, with rugged twisted trunks. Blush pink buds expand to soft white blooms.

a broader form, with an egg-shaped or even a globe-shaped crown.

Five basic types of tree form are recognized: (1) conical, essentially a narrow tree with a prominent leader; (2) ovoid or egg-shaped with broader spreading branches and rounded summit; (3) spherical or globe-shaped with spreading branches forming a dome; (4) broad-spreading or flat-topped with practically horizontal branches, and (5) arching crown with branches bowed at their extremities. The color plates illustrate these basic forms very clearly. Of course, trees rarely fit these patterns precisely.

Innumerable modifications of the fundamental patterns may be seen among trees. The horse-chestnut is characteristically a globe-shaped tree whose branches droop but finally turn upward at the tips. Erect or up-sweeping branches create an aspiring effect. Cornelian-cherry, saucer magnolia and Chinese dogwood, in the younger stages, possess this trait to a remarkable degree. The horizontal lines which predominate in the flowering and giant dogwoods, the Japanese snowbell and the blackhaw suggest repose. Melancholy is the principal impression aroused by flowering trees with pendent branches, such as the rosebud cherry. Sometimes I can see a frozen waterfall or fountain in trees with pendent branches. Can you?

21

FLOWERING TREES

Beauty From Bark and Twig

In winter, deciduous trees reveal beauty, strength and structure of bark and branchlet not noticed while they were in foliage. In the vicinity of New York City, the leafless season extends for six or seven months. If gardens and landscapes are to sustain interest then, tree features such as branches and bark color patterns are important.

Fundamental to trees is the stem or trunk that raises their leaves toward the light, the better to catch the sun's life-giving rays. A sturdy trunk is beautiful in itself, and it supports and sustains the great weight of not only the branches but also the leaves, flowers and fruits that they bear each successive year. But the color and sculpturing of bark, the play of light over its columnar surface are subtler pleasing qualities. The smooth gray trunk of the beechlike yellowwood, when the low rays of sunlight play upon it from the side, provides a glimpse of beauty and strength among trees.

The principal function of bark is to protect the living layer of plant tissue (cambium) that is found just beneath its surface. Bark is frequently tough. It assumes different patterns and colors, varying to species and age. Except for lenticels (tiny wartlike specks or streaks) the bark of twigs is usually smooth. As the branch increases in thickness

22

the outer covering usually cracks, forming vertical ridges and furrows. Nevertheless, the branches and stems of some trees do not rupture but remain smooth throughout the life of the tree.

The flowering dogwood, black-haw, and sourwood have trunk bark which becomes checkered into thick plates, like alligator hide. Black locust, silverbell and tulip-tree have thick furrowed bark that forms long ridges along the trunk. Smooth bark is seen in several ornamental species of flowering trees many of which develop a rough bark on the main stem in later years. Magnolias, service-berry and yellowwood retain a permanently smooth outer covering.

New leaves arise each year on an axis called a twig or branchlet. It may be six to twelve or more inches long, depending upon its position and the species. Most flowering trees bear buds in the axils of these leaves plus a larger one at the twig's end.

The large bud at the tip of the shoot is responsible for prolonging the axis. Lateral buds near the tip usually develop into branches. Not all buds however, become active. This helps to give individuality to each species.

Vigor of shoot has much to do with vividness of winter color among flowering trees. First-year shoots are often highly colored. These branchlets form a peripheral zone over the crown of the tree. If individual shoots are long they present a large surface of color. Korean dogwood has red shoots; shoots of the scholar-tree and sweetbay magnolia are green. Twig color effects can be accentuated by pruning or by the application of fertilizer to stimulate shoot length.

BUDS

The small structures at the tips of tree twigs and along the shoots are buds, the vital points from which new growth rises each year. These are usually capped by hard and shiny or hairy overlapping scales. Sometimes only a heavy feltlike material covers the leaf buds or flower buds. Frequently buds are conspicuous on account of size or shape, color, gloss, or covering.

Buds tell a fascinating story to those who are able to read their meaning. The bud represents a resting stage in the life of the tree, a period in which the plant passes a season unfavorable to growth. Three types of buds may be recognized: (1) the shoot or vegetative bud, (2) the flower bud and (3) the mixed shoot and flower bud. It is sometimes possible to predict a tree's bloom by observing the flower buds or shortage of them. You learn

2. The nodding, hairy buds of the Empress-tree burst into glorious lavender trumpets before the leaves unfold in May.

25

by experience. Mixed buds are likely to be somewhat larger than shoot buds and they may be slightly hairy. The embryonic flowers may be seen by slicing a bud carefully with a sharp knife.

4

Handsome Horizontals in Dogwoods

It would not be spring without the dogwoods. The gaiety of the season is accented by the purity of the white (or reddish) blossoms which open before the leaves unfold. Dogwoods, however, are attractive throughout the year. Late April to early May is the height of the blossom season for the Eastern flowering dogwood.

The blooms arise from swollen buds borne at the tips of short shoots. The four large "petals" of the "flower" actually are bracts or scales that enclose the flower during the winter (Illustration 3). These coverings grow by expanding from the region of attachment, blanching as they enlarge, until the white "blossoms" reach a size of three to five inches across. The true flowers are the insignificant greenish parts in the center, at the hub of the

3. Four notched white "petals" garland the tight clusters of tiny yellow florets on America's Eastern Flowering Dogwood in early spring; petals are actually expanded bud scales that blanch as they develop.

petals (much like the bracts and flowers of the Christmas poinsettia).

Eastern Species

The Eastern flowering dogwood, *Cornus florida,* is a small tree about fifteen or twenty feet high having tier upon tier of flattened branches terminating in bulbous flower buds. Branchlets arise in clusters near the end of each shoot. One of these twigs outgrows the others to increase the length of the branch. Since this branchlet is not the tipmost and it grows in a sweeping arc, the branches of flowering dogwood, like those of the sassafras, are undulating in silhouette. When the tree is young the branches are ascending, but as maturity approaches the branches gradually develop a horizontal position.

Planting distance between two flowering dogwoods should be at least twenty feet (less than that for one dogwood, if its nearest neighbor is a house or a non-spreading tree). Even though young trees may appear to be lost at this interval, their branches soon spread out to occupy the space. The roots of dogwoods are close to the soil surface. Few types of low-growing plants can be set out beneath them, for the roots offer strong competition. Hay-scented ferns and May-apple are aggressive enough to prosper there. Periwinkle *(Vinca minor)* or pachysan-

29

dra succeed also. The low-spreading Japanese azaleas may be tried but bloom is likely to be sparse owing to the deep shade during summer.

Eastern flowering dogwood is sensitive to drought. When the weather is sunny, hot and dry, let the hose soak the soil beneath the tree's branches. If a shortage of soil moisture becomes critical, dogwood leaves turn brown along the edges. This is a sign of distress that persists as an unsightly blemish for the duration of the summer. A wood-chip mulch helps to keep soil cool and moist. Inspect the mulch for mice in autumn, lest the hungry animals hide under it while gnawing the dogwood's tender bark when no other food source is convenient.

Autumn Action

Early in autumn the dogwood berries ripen; they are bunched into tight clusters. For a brief period the green foliage contrasts beautifully with the bright red fruits. Soon the leaves assume brilliant hues of flame and scarlet to rival the sour gum, sumac and sassafras. The undersides of the leaves are paler than the upper surfaces. This contrast is pleasing especially when the foliage is in motion. Migrating birds, notably robins and cedar waxwings, gobble the red shiny berries shortly after the crop has ripened. Thus this phase of the dogwood's beauty is usually fleeting, so enjoy it as it occurs. We would not deprive songbirds of fair forage, especially when we realize what they do in summer to control ravaging insects.

Bark borer is likely to attack weakened trees. Watch for tiny holes near the base of the trunk. Little mounds of sawdust may also indicate their presence. Probe the tunnels with a pliable wire or apply an anti-borer fumigant (obtainable at garden supply shops) and then plug the ports with chewing gum.

Petal blight, reported chiefly in the South, mars the dogwood floral display during wet seasons. A fungicide sprayed on the petals just as they turn white should check this disease.

If your apparently healthy, well-established dogwood consistently fails to flower or has an erratic blooming habit, or produces disfigured flowers, the fault may lie in winterkilling of flower buds. If you are not willing to accept this in some seasons, move the tree to a less exposed location.

Several novelties of *Cornus florida* are available: variety *rubra,* a pink-flowered form; 'Pluribracteata,' a so-called double flowering form; 'Pendula,' with pendent branches, and 'Welchii,' with colored-foliage.

FLOWERING TREES

In the West

From British Columbia to California the Pacific dog-wood, *Cornus Nuttallii,* is found as an understory tree in the coniferous forests. It is larger than the Eastern flowering species, attaining heights of fifty feet in nature. The petals are broader, up to six inches across, and more numerous, usually six. Also, the flowers appear during two seasons, spring and fall. In the fall, the white bracts are conspicuous as the fruits from the first blooms are turning red. All this takes place in a setting of the somber green of needled evergreens. Unfortunately for Eastern gardeners, the Pacfic dogwood is not adapted to the rigors of the drier colder climate and consequently is not to be seen in the East in its natural glory. Curiously, the Eastern dogwood languishes when taken to Europe.

Chinese Dogwood

The flowering dogwood, *Cornus Kousa,* of eastern Asia develops its spectacular white floral bracts about one month after the native species has gone by. The oriental species differs from the American species in its pointed bracts which expand after the leaves have unfolded. The effect is that of a snowstorm in summer covering the leafy branches in a blanket of white. Young specimens do not bloom for several years, but the patient gardener is eventually and abundantly rewarded by a yearly profusion of flowers.

In American gardens, the oriental flowering dogwood attains a height of about fifteen feet. It has a low forked trunk with flaky bark and a broad, spreading, rather flat-topped crown. In youth this small tree assumes a wine-glass form. Long slender branches tipped by pointed dark buds ascend at a steep angle from the smooth trunk. As with the American species, this flowering dogwood requires a twenty-foot planting interval between trees.

Korean Dogwood

For an asymmetrical dogwood with the picturesque Japanese form, I suggest the rarely seen Korean dogwood, *Cornus coreana,* with persimmon-type bark and a tortuous stem that rises to a height of twenty feet. The branchlets are reddish brown becoming purplish as the season advances. Flower clusters measure up to three inches across. The berries ripen bluish purple.

Cornelian-cherry (Dogwood)

Europe's contribution among dogwood trees is *Cornus mas,* the cornelian-cherry, actually a dogwood with red cherrylike fruits that ripen during the cherry season

33

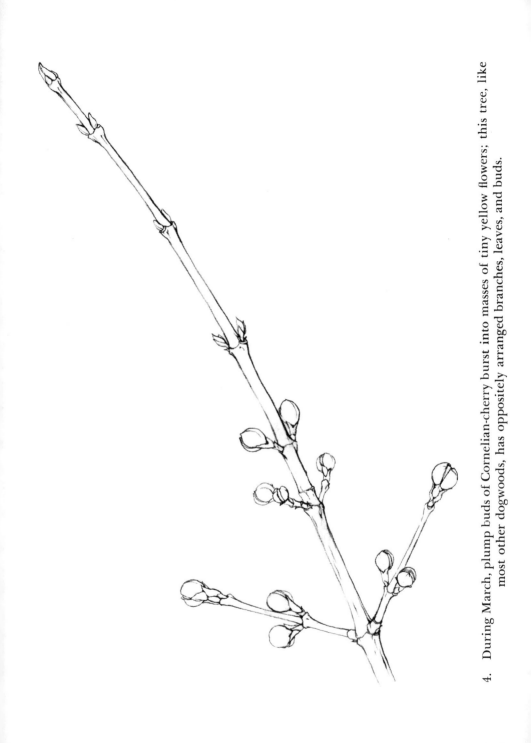

4. During March, plump buds of Cornelian-cherry burst into masses of tiny yellow flowers; this tree, like most other dogwoods, has oppositely arranged branches, leaves, and buds.

(Illustration 4). These "cherries" differ from the orchard varieties by their shape (which is elongated), their short stalk and their flavor (which is tart). The fruits make excellent jelly if you can gather them before the birds do. During the brief season in July that they hang amid the luxurious foliage, they create a beautiful contrast of scarlet and green. This small tree is closely related to the bunch-berry, or cornel, of northern forests, a creeping dwarf shrub of the same dogwood family.

Cornelian-cherry may be grown with a single stem through selection and early training. It reaches ten to fifteen feet and eventually becomes a round-headed small tree with spreading branches from a low trunk, although in youth the branches are decidedly upsweeping. In earliest spring, after the first few warm days, the branches become thickly set with small bunches of misty yellow flowers. Complimented by the reddish branches, the yellow blossom clusters have a subtler hue than the boisterous golden bells of forsythia. The cornelian-cherry's flowers, which are bunched into small bouquets, arise from conspicuous buds borne on short spurs. The floral display carries its message of hope for several weeks, if April's weather remains chilly.

The leaves of all dogwoods have arching veins and the margins are without teeth. Leaves of the cornelian-

35

cherry are small, measuring up to two and one-half inches in length. The upper surface is glossy. In autumn the leaves become reddish before falling late in the season.

A similar species from eastern Asia is the Japanese cornelian-cherry, *Cornus officinalis,* which may be distinguished by the upsweep of the branches. In the European species the branches are jointed between the yearly growths while in the oriental species they are curved.

Giant Dogwood

Dogwood trees with leaves arranged alternately are unusual. One such is the pagoda dogwood, *Cornus alternifolia,* also called blue dogwood or pigeonberry. This is the native species that reaches its greatest development in elevated sites of the Appalachian mountains. Unfortunately, for all its beauty in nature, it does not take kindly to cultivation. A better choice, therefore, is the so-called giant dogwood of China and Japan, *Cornus controversa,* the Asiatic counterpart of the pagoda dogwood.

This giant dogwood grows to fifteen or twenty feet and the branches, which spread an equal width, create the pagoda effect, since they are disposed in symmetrical horizontal tiers. Tiny white flowers borne in flat clusters up to two inches across appear along the horizontal branches as the leaves unfold in late May and early June. The leaves, which are not quite opposite and which arise close together toward the tips of the shoots, measure between three and five inches long. In autumn the leaves turn purplish red. The dark blue fruits are gathered by birds, leaving the barren reddish fruit stalks standing like candelabras.

The giant dogwood forms a symmetrical small tree that may be grown as a free standing specimen at the edge of a lawn. The lower branches should be allowed to develop naturally and to sweep the turf. A well-drained upland site in sun is ideal. A shady location would produce an open habit and decrease the floral attractiveness.

5

Crabapple Means Landscape Loveliness

Apple blossoms—just those two words conjure a parade of delicious memories but gardeners who grow the lovely flowering crabapples of today have their own storehouse of memories and anticipations. Modern crabapples are ornamentals from Asia. Flowers are more showy than those of the commercial cultivated apple varieties. Instead of fading flesh-pink petals on short woolly stalks, crabapples offer finely colorful flowers, with some varieties fragrant, borne on long slender stalks, the petals often being doubled in number.

Crabapples—various species of the genus *Malus*—are among the progenitors of the luscious orchard apples (various forms of one species, *Malus pumila*). And it was from the small-fruited types that farmers raised the juicy highly colored and flavorful giants that give us pies and cider. In branch structure and silhouette, the crabapple tree develops on the same pattern as the cultivated apple but its branches are less rugged than those of its orchard cousin. The crabapple is better fitted for the intimacy of the private garden. A rounded crown is the rule, although some sorts are vertically oblong; others are even shaped like a wine glass, flaring out from a low forked trunk. In stature some ultimately grow to thirty-five or forty feet and spread an equal distance. They produce delicate but prolific bloom along sturdy, slender, spreading or arching branches. Their notable red or yellow fruits are less than two inches in diameter.

Crabapples, like other members of the rose family, perform best in a sunny site with well-drained soil. They need a dormant oil spray in late March, just before the buds break. The tent caterpillar must be guarded against in late April.

The blooming season of any particular crabapple species extends for about ten days, while, for the group as a whole, with overlappings, it may cover nearly a month in the vicinity of New York City—from late April to mid-May—depending upon the weather. Most apples bloom profusely one year and sparsely the succeeding year, a natural habit. The flowers are numerous, borne six to nine in a cluster, and are usually pink in bud. In many sorts they fade to blush pink or white as they expand but one class retains a purplish red color.

POPULAR SPECIES

A most dependable sort is the Japanese flowering crab, *Malus floribunda* (Color Plate I), which has wide-spreading wavy branches set with many twigs. The flower clusters arise on these short spurs and produce a fleecy cloud effect early in the crabapple blooming season. Unfolding buds are bright pink. The pink fades to blush as the petals expand. Blooms appear in great profusion year after year, hence the name floribunda. The blossoms are followed in autumn by abundant small apples. Migrating and winter birds work at this ample storehouse, so that by spring no trace of last year's fruit remains except possibly an occasional slender fruit stalk.

Malus floribunda comes to us from Japanese gardens. Its parentage, a mystery, may only be inferred. The stature is from twelve to fifteen feet. In maturity the branches become spreading and the scaffold branches, clothed in scaly bark, often assume curiously gnarled attitudes from a low trunk. This tree is at its best as a freestanding specimen on the lawn.

A wine-glass-shaped small tree with long stiff branches

40

festooned with many petaled blush "roses" is the Scheidecker crabapple, *Malus Scheideckeri*. Combine these features with a delicate fresh fragrance and the effect is exquisite. In bud the enlarging petals are blush pink. As they expand to full-bloom roselike flowers they reveal a pale, soft, gray texture. The petals, which vary from ten to twenty in number, are pink streaked on the underside.

This fifteen-foot tree has low branches forming a V silhouette. The long, diverging branches are studded with spurs disposed in such a manner that the branch is entirely encircled with foliage. The apples are medium sized, red or yellow and tipped by the five-lobed calyx. This variety was introduced by the Scheidecker Nursery in Germany in 1888.

An arching small tree scarcely ten feet tall with large white fragrant flowers, bright pink in bud on long red stalks, is the Arnold crabapple, *Malus Arnoldiana*. It arose as a seedling in an inaccessible border of the Arnold Arboretum in Jamaica Plain, Massachusetts, about 1883. What an exquisite flowering small tree is this crabapple, entirely suited for the border or as a free standing specimen in a restricted space. Its parentage is inferred to be *Malus floribunda* $\times$ *Malus baccata*.

The tea crabapple, *Malus hupehensis*, is a five-petaled

fragrant crabapple whose buds are bright pink, borne on dark red stems. When full blown the petals become white. As with the Scheidecker crabapple, the tea crab is characterized by great wands of flowers on its diverging branches. It also bears flowers in alternate years, but the form of the branching is so distinctive that you will want to grow it despite its off-again-on-again blooming habit. The fruits are small, red cherrylike apples on long red stalks. The young plants come true from seed, a unique quality among crabapples. Foliage is reddish while unfolding. The vase shape of young plants is lost in age when established trees develop wide-spreading branches. Height is seldom greater than eighteen feet. This species would also look well in a shrub border.

A choice flowering tree whose expanding buds resemble miniature pink rosebuds is the Chinese flowering crabapple, *Malus spectabilis,* with white full-blown blooms. This is an old variety that came out of Chinese gardens centuries ago. A form with larger, pinker buds was first grown in England in 1872; called 'Riversii,' it has more and larger petals. When young, the tree is vase shaped. As it develops, the crown becomes rounded so that at the height of bloom it would suggest a giant snowball (if its lower structure could be concealed). It may be planted in virtually any prominent situation, either to combine and compliment other crabapples, or with its glistening white flowers in contrast to the foliage of evergreens.

NOTABLE VARIETIES

An outstanding pink crabapple is 'Dorothea,' introduced by the Arnold Arboretum. Shy in growing, nevertheless it is so appealing that it is certain to find increasing favor in gardens. The bright pink petals become whitish along the central axis while remaining soft pink toward the edge. The effect is velvety in pastel tones. This spreading small tree will be a center of attention during the blooming season no matter where it is situated.

In ten years, 'Dorothea,' with normal good culture, will reach six to seven feet with an equal spread. The bark is smooth reddish gray with showy creamy dots scattered along the new shoots. The branching pattern is open. When this crabapple blooms each year the long branches become bright pink wands. The fruits are tiny yellow apples.

'Katherine,' discovered among seedlings at Rochester, New York, in 1928 by the distinguished plantsman, Bernard H. Slavin, bears the name of his daughter-in-law. The double glistening white flowers recall the Chinese flowering crab. Twenty pinkish petals expand into a bloom that becomes more than two inches across. These flowers are spaced about the branch so as to form a festooned wand. The smooth green flower stalks are surmounted by a large greenish receptacle with a reddish cheek and vertical red markings. The filaments of the numerous stamens are white, accentuating the purity of the flower.

The deepest pink and the most delicate flowers among crabapples occur in the Parkman crab, *Malus Halliana* 'Parkmanii.' The blooms are so heavy for the smooth long red stems that they are nodding. This variety needs a protected site for best performance. It is a small tree with smooth slender gray barked twiggy branches that arch in all directions. Pruning will improve its form.

AMERICAN CRABAPPLES

Among the American species—those that unfold with large clear pink petals—are the double-flowered forms *Malus coronaria* 'Charlottae' and *Malus ioensis* 'Prince Georges.' The American crabapples are later blooming and so extend the season, but they are especially prone to attack by cedar-apple rust fungus. The gardener is faced with the choice between growing red cedar trees or crabapples. Each species alternates as a host for the rust fungus, which forms large warty gall-like structures on red cedar, and midsummer leaf blemishes on the crabapple. If red cedars are plentiful in your vicinity, then you have no choice—you must find a substitute for the crabapple's pink flowers. (Also fire-blight bacterial disease is sometimes troublesome.)

Earliest to Bloom

Among the earliest-blooming crabapples are the Siberian crabs, *Malus baccata,* which appear while the long stalked, light green leaves are unfolding. Pale pink in bud, these flowers expand to glistening white in large cup-shaped blooms, usually on smooth slender stalks. Fragrance is fresh and delicate. The foliage is distinctive in its elliptical shape and thin texture. The variety 'Gracilis,' grown from seed collected by William Purdom in China about 1910, has graceful branches and an arching habit. The fruits are reddish, small, and sought after by birds. Height of a mature tree is about forty feet, so that it could replace the traditional apple on terraces where ample shade for outdoor living is desired.

The peach-leaf crabapple, *Malus robusta* 'Persicifolia,' akin to the Siberian species, is a hybrid derived from it and the pear-leaf crabapple, *Malus prunifolia.* Flowers are white, borne on long ascending, spreading branches.

The distinction of this species is the leaf shape. It may be used in a border where the foliage can contrast with neighboring leaf patterns. Fruits are red or yellow, small, and may or may not be tipped by the calyx teeth.

The cutleaf crabapple, *Malus toringoides,* is an upright medium-sized tree with three-lobed leaves that assume brilliant autumn coloration. As with the American crabs, however, it ought not to be planted near red cedars, since it is subject to cedar-apple rust that blemishes the leaves. The elongated fruits with bright colored cheeks are distinctive. Outer branches cascade from an eighteen-foot tree that spreads twelve feet.

Red Fountain, a so-called weeping crabapple, 'Red Jade,' introduced by the Brooklyn Botanic Garden, has flowers of white and fruits of glistening red. Branchlets are so delicate and graceful that they are pendent. Not the front lawn but rather a position above a wall is the best situation for this fountain-like floral effect.

For a dwarf spreading tree the Sargent crabapple, *Malus Sargentii,* is suggested. If the lower branches are permitted to sweep the ground, the effect is that of a large, wide-spreading, low-growing shrub. The single stem shows that it is truly a tree. It was first considered a dwarf variety of the Toringo crabapple, *Malus Sieboldii,* to which it bears a striking resemblance. Buds are creamy, developing into white almost circular petals when fully expanded. These are disposed in a plane about the yellow anthers.

The Carmine crab, *Malus atrosanguinea,* is popular because of its myriad bright orange-red flowers early in the crabapple season. The small blooms are borne in such profusion that the wide-spreading tree appears to be completely covered. Care must be given to its position in the landscape, because this tree's striking flower color dominates the landscape. It is best displayed against the dark neutral background of conifers.

Among the earliest-to-flower yet the most difficult to use in the landscape is the purple crabapple, *Malus purpurea,* with rosy magenta flowers and reddish foliage. As a specimen this tree is exquisite. But a garden scene is a composition—a blend of shadow, shapes and colors. Purple-leaved plants cannot be used just anywhere. However if the picture calls for such a color note, the deepest-colored form is Lemoine's crabapple, *Malus purpurea* 'Lemoinei.' A white-flowering crabapple could be planted nearby, to soften the dull magenta of this purple variety.

6

Magnolia for Magnificence

Far away places and tropical luxuriance come to mind when the sweet-scented, large, creamy white blooms of the magnolia expand in the warm days of springtime and early summer. Evening brings out the delicious perfume of the huge flowers. White predominates in this group. Pinks and pale and deep rose to purplish colors also have much to recommend them. There is even a yellow form available. Depending upon the species, the flowers range from about three inches to sometimes as much as a foot across.

The simple flower, consisting of numerous petals and stamens surrounding a conelike axis containing numerous carpels, is considered by botanists to be a basic and very ancient type. In ages past, when climates were moderate over a more extensive area, magnolia ancestors were world wide in their distribution. Since glacial times they have become restricted in large measure to tropical and warmer temperate regions of the northern hemisphere.

Nearly thirty-five species or horticultural varieties are being cultivated. Many of these have arisen as seedlings of species brought into gardens. There are nine native species and sixteen from eastern Asia. In general, the oriental sorts bloom before the leaves unfold, whereas the flowers of the American ones appear with the foliage or soon afterwards. Most species are deciduous; a few are evergreen. The flowers, borne terminally on shoots of the previous season, arise from buds having but a single scale. The group is dedicated to the memory of Pierre Magnol, 1638-1715, one-time director of the Montpellier Botanic Garden.

Among early spring-blooming trees, the magnolia occupies center stage for its breathtaking loveliness. In gardens of the temperate zone, it is without rival for size of flower and size of undivided leaf. Certain of the oriental members have hairy buds that unfold to reveal exquisite pink and white flowers with fine fragrance. One could not wish for more.

5. Fleshy strap-like petals decorate the naked gray branches of the Star Magnolia in earliest springtime. Locate the tree in an exposed situation to retard blooming if you want to be sure the flowers will not be killed by frost.

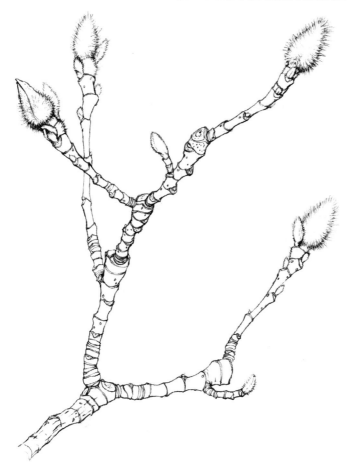

6.   Woolly flower buds tip the smooth gray twigs of Star Magnolia through winter months; in earliest spring the fuzzy caps split open when the white petals expand.

51

FLOWERING TREES

Early and Late

The multi-stemmed, white-flowered star magnolia, *Magnolia Kobus* variety *stellata*, with ribbonlike petals, is the first to open over most of the Middle-Atlantic area in April (Illustration 5 and 6). The combination of early flowering and late frost will spoil its bloom about once every four or five years. However, some buds usually survive and, besides, to most Easterners the floral display in other years is compensation. The rosy flowered form, 'Rosea,' also is exquisite. The low stature of this species makes it ideal for many situations around modern one-story and split-level homes.

The Kobus magnolia, *Magnolia Kobus* (Illustration 7), displays broad cup-shaped white petals in earliest spring. In stature the shrublike tree reaches twenty to twenty-five feet. It is hardy but often takes many years before it blooms regularly.

Spectacular with large bell-shaped fragrant flowers is the Yulan magnolia, *Magnolia denudata* (or *M. conspicua*). As a free-standing maturing specimen, this symmetrical plant is handsome in bloom. And it blooms as early as the second or third year. The white petals, nine in number, are almost fleshy, and are indistinguishable from the sepals. The tree is capable of attaining forty

II. Purple flowered Lennei Magnolia makes a charming accent in the intimate
garden. Flowers of Oriental magnolias adorn naked branches in early spring.

7. The Kobus Magnolia with its pure white petals is among the first flowering trees to unfold in spring; circular scars in the crotch indicate the position of the flower two years earlier.

53

8. Attractive flowers make the Saucer Magnolia among the most popular of springtime trees. The expanding flower succeeds an earlier bloom which falls, revealing a developing cone.

9. The unfolding purplish petals of the Lennei Magnolia reveal pale, rose pink inner surfaces. Compared to other Oriental Magnolias, its bloom is late, but it has one of the deepest colors of springtime trees.

feet, so that ample room must be allowed for its full development.

Shades of pink to purple are among the merits of the popular and hardy saucer magnolia, *Magnolia Soulangiana,* (also spelled Soulangeana, although the "i" spelling is standard with authorities such as Alfred Rehder). It is a hybrid between *M. denudata* and *M. liliflora,* both of Asiatic origin. It occurred in the garden of the Chevalier Soulange-Bodin at Fromont near Paris in the early nineteenth century. Flowers are bell-shaped, scarcely resembling a saucer except when fully blown and they measure four to six inches across (Illustration 8). Sepals are half as long as petals. Colors range from pinkish white to rosy purple in a beautifully graded series between the parents. Several named forms are available, the most popular one being 'Lennei,' a late-flowering form with deep rose-purple petals (Color Plate IV, Illustration 9).

Fragrant Blossoms

A symmetrical species with small leaves, but which often requires many years before it blooms, is the anise magnolia, *Magnolia salicifolia.* Although the leaves suggest the willow, the common name has been derived from the scent of anise that arises from a crushed leaf or broken twig.

In June the sweetbay (or swampbay), *Magnolia virginiana,* produces its delicately scented cup-shaped blooms and continues sporadically throughout the summer. This species abounds in low, poorly drained spots on the Atlantic coastal plain as far north as Cape Cod. Leaves are oblong and glaucous beneath. Stems arise from a clump as a shrub and branches are short and green. Some leaves usually persist until the New Year, but it is a deciduous plant in the North. In the South it attains tree-like dimensions.

The bullbay or evergreen magnolia, *Magnolia grandiflora,* is a striking evergreen in the South where it reaches eighty feet or more. Leaves are large, thick, glossy above, rusty beneath and persist throughout the year. Flowers are creamy white, appearing in midsummer with a lemony scent. Several selections have been made by nurserymen. In northern gardens the bullbay needs a bit of pampering. If the site is well drained and not too fertile, and if the plant receives protection from winter wind and sunshine, then it is likely to succeed in gardens along the coast as far north as Long Island and Cape Cod.

Pruning of magnolias cannot be done except on young branchlets since the bark does not readily heal; therefore

keep your eye sharp for the early development of unwanted shoots. Remove them promptly. Spring planting
is definitely recommended; moving a tree when it is in
bloom often gives superior results. Tulip scale is the
only insect pest which is likely to attack magnolias. This
can be controlled by an oil spray applied in late winter.
With the principal exception of *M. virginiana,* the magnolias generally do best in well-drained soil.

7

Cherries for Mists of White and Pink

There is a charm about delicate cherry blossoms on slender red stalks that draws us irresistibly toward the trees, the better to admire their beauty. Though spring skies are dark, the air is crisp when the first cherries burst into bloom, and despite inclement weather, cherry blossoms always carry the promise of another gardening year.

Cherries, with almonds, peaches and plums, are major members of the genus *Prunus* (of the rose family). About two hundred species of *Prunus* are found in temperate regions of the northern hemisphere plus a few species in the Andes. Those with edible fruits are cultivated in orchards. Many species are grown ornamentally. Blooms are usually borne in clusters, depending upon the species, and may be rose, pink or white, double or single.

Petals are in fives or a multiple up to thirty and more. Double-flowered sorts expand just before leaves unfold. Against reddish or black branches, the effect is that of a pink snowstorm or of a cloud floating low in the landscape.

Flowering cherries are welcome garden ornaments owing to their floriferous early color that transforms a thicket of branches into soft loveliness. The blooming season may extend for two weeks—if temperatures are moderate. In the garden an assortment of species of this group may provide color for six weeks, starting in early April with the purple-leaved plum, *Prunus cerasifera* 'Pissardii,' followed by the rosebud or weeping Higan cherry, *P. subhirtella* variety *pendula* (Color Plate III), the Yoshino cherry, *P. yedoensis,* the mountain cherry, *P. Sargentii,* the Fuji cherry, *P. incisa,* the peach, *P. Persica,* the oriental flowering cherry, *P. serrulata* in variety, the beach plum, *P. maritima* and the wild black cherry, *P. serotina.*

Note that with the oriental flowering cherries there is no nuisance of birds bickering for the fruits, since they are borne very sparingly, if at all. Some of the other sorts —cherries, plums, apricots—do develop fruit, but it would scarcely repay the home gardener to nurture them

60

just for fruit when commercial orchards today offer fruit of such fine quality.

The generally fine-textured foliage of cherries is well colored in shades of green, more or less glossy. Even though the large-leaved Japanese cherries have such closely toothed margins, the overall effect is one of refinement. In autumn, some sorts assume deep vinous hues. The bark is attractive at all seasons with its reddish glossy smoothness interrupted by the horizontal ridges of lenticels. The large, pointed buds with reddish scales are conspicuous throughout winter.

According to species, cherry trees are small to medium in size, usually with spreading branches. Some are upright while a few are pendent, traits that make them admirable trees for the home landscape. Planted for ornament, cherries require little care but they are subject to attacks by tent caterpillar. These can be controlled by disrupting the webs with a broom just as the leaf buds are opening or by squirting a solution of oil and kerosene into the nests.

Japanese Flowering Cherries
Prunus serrulata forms

Cultivated by the Japanese for hundreds of years, the Japanese flowering cherries symbolize beauty and are a

61

national flower of Japan. Stories are told among the Japanese of the fairy maiden who causes trees to bloom by hovering low in the spring sky, awakening the sleeping cherry trees to life with her delicate breath.

The names which the Japanese have bestowed on cherry trees bespeak the esteem in which certain varieties are held: *Shiro-fugen* in English becomes "white goddess," *Sirotae* is "snow white," and *Amanogawa* refers to river of the sky, hence the "milky way." *Fugenzo*, known for more than five hundred years, may be translated "goddess on a white elephant," while *Shogetsu* means "moon hanging low by a pine tree."

"In very early times," writes Paul Russell,* "only the wild single-flowered cherries were known, but as these were brought under cultivation in the gardens of wealthy Japanese nobles, flowers with extra petals and of larger size began to appear. The tendency toward variation, which is particularly strong in the oriental cherries, was greatly accelerated and stimulated by more favorable growing conditions. As these different forms arose, the better ones were assembled at the imperial gardens at Kyoto, in temple gardens, and in the gardens of a few wealthy nobles."

* Paul Russell was formerly a botanist for the Office of Foreign Plant Introduction, Bureau of Plant Industry, U.S. Department of Agriculture.

The most famous of American collections, without doubt, is the fifty-year-old planting in Potomac Park at Washington, D.C. In 1912, the Honorable Yukio Azaki, mayor of Tokyo, presented more than two thousand trees as a gift of friendship from the city of Tokyo to the city of Washington. The early-blooming single-flowered trees of this collection encircling the Tidal Basin are the Yoshino cherry, while the several forms of *Prunus serrulata,* which extend the season to about a month, are planted along East and West Drives.

The Rochester nursery firm of Ellwanger and Barry offered *"Cerasus pendula*—pretty, round, dense head with slender weeping branches"—in 1846. Parsons & Co. of Flushing offered *"Cerasus pendula plena"* in 1852—the first double-flowering cherry available in America. The United States Department of Agriculture's office of foreign plant introductions in 1903, received a consignment of some thirty named varieties from its agents in Japan. These and later U.S.D.A. importations are the principal ancestors of the more than fifty Japanese flowering cherry varieties presently available in American nurseries.

Japanese flowering cherries offer bloom that ranges from deep pink to white with petals numbering five, called "single," to as many as thirty, called "double." Flowers are borne singly or up to six in a cluster. Individual blooms measure from somewhat over one inch to as much as two and one half inches across. Single types have the advantage of fragrance and early blooming, while double forms remain in bloom for a longer period.

A major consideration in selecting these cherries for your home property is their adaptability to American gardens, especially northern ones. In the East, the vicinity of Portland, Maine, seems to be the northernmost limit near the coast where the Japanese cherries will grow. A big problem is establishment. After the first few years, trees seem to outgrow their tenderness. Take precautions to avoid late growth in summer. Do not irrigate after Labor Day; apply no fertilizer after Memorial Day, use a mulch over the roots to conserve moisture and keep the soil cool. Japanese flowering cherries may be safely planted wherever peaches are grown successfully. Southern limits occur where cherries are subjected to a prolonged growing season so that the plants do not have a chance to become dormant before freezing weather.

Fragrance is pronounced in the single-flowered varieties, and it is well to include at least one tree with scented flowers in your planting. Flowering cherries are displayed to advantage in small groups against needled evergreens where the neutral green foliage provides a background for the bright cloud of flowers.

SOME FAVORITE VARIETIES

Of the numerous varieties available, there are a few distinctive ones worth including in a small garden. If space is not a factor, an assortment is most desirable. There are several categories, according to flower and tree form. The most popular group is the pink, double-flowering Japanese cherries.

'Kwanzan,' a cherry commemorating a mountain in Japan, is a vigorous variety with the darkest double pink blooms of the oriental flowering cherries. Three to five blooms borne in pendulous clusters, each flower measuring up to two and one half inches across, may have as many as thirty petals. At Harms Point in Potomac Park, Washington, more than two hundred mature trees may be seen. In about fifty years they have attained rounded crowns some twenty feet high. The branches are spreading.

'Shogetsu' is a fifteen-foot tree with a broad flat crown. The deep rose-pink buds unfold into blooms of about thirty petals, pale pink at the margins and almost white at the center. Up to two inches across, they hang in clusters of three to six. When partly open, blooms suggest the double form of English daisy.

'Fugenzo,' also double-flowered, has been known for

more than five hundred years, according to Dr. Manbu Miyoshi, former director of the Tokyo Botanic Garden. Introduced into England in 1892 by the Veitch nursery, this one is sometimes called "James Veitch." Paul Russell states that it is "not very common in this country," often being confused with 'Shiro-fugen.' The tree at eighteen feet attains a flattened crown with intertwining branches. The deep rose-hued expanding flower buds are protected by characteristically narrow curled sepals. The four to six blooms open successively, forming a compact bouquet. Individual flowers measure up to two inches with thirty rose-pink petals which, with age, grow pale but never white. The aging flowers of 'Shiro-fugen' in contrast become glistening white. 'Fugenzo' blooms at the same time as 'Kwanzan' and retains the pale rose-pink color.

'Sirotae' is a white double-flowered variety that may grow to twenty-five feet. The wide-spreading branches rise from a short trunk. Blooms measure up to two inches and have about twelve petals with two to five flowers in somewhat nodding clusters.

'Amanogawa' refers to "river of the sky" or the "milky way." "When this tree is seen in full bloom against a dark background," writes Paul Russell, "the appropriateness of the Japanese name is readily comprehended."

The light-pink blooms are semidouble, that is, with up to fifteen petals and they measure up to one and three-fourths inches across, they are borne in stiff upright clusters of usually three blooms. 'Tanabata' is a white-flowered form but it is doubtful if it is available outside of Japan. 'Amanogawa' was introduced to this country in 1906 by Dr. David Fairchild, at that time a plant explorer for the United States Department of Agriculture.

'Oshima-zakura' is the form found on the Island of Oshima at the entrance to Sagami Sea in the outer harbor of Tokyo. Some botanists hold that, because of a combination of shared characters such as bark color, leaf margins and flower fragrance, this species is one of the parents of many of the double-flowered Japanese cherries. 'Oshima-zakura' suggests that many horticultural plants in the distant past were brought into gardens from the wild, and in certain instances bred with related plants, thus becoming parents of improved or domestic varieties. 'Taihaku-zakura,' the "great white cherry," is an example. At the beginning of the twentieth century this variety was sent to England as an unnamed seedling. It is considered the finest of the white single-flowered Japanese cherries. At the suggestion of Prince Taka Tsukasa, Collingwood Ingram of Benendon, Kent in England, gave it a Japanese name. It is a vigorous tree with blooms up to two and one-half inches across in clusters of two or three blooms.

'Jo-nioi,' meaning supreme fragrance, is a tree that reaches eighteen feet and has a broad crown. The slender flower buds are pinkish and the expanding petals, one and one-half inches across, are white. Exquisite fragrance is the principal asset.

Earlier-blooming Asiatic cherries to extend the blooming season include varieties from four species; the Higan (equinox) cherry and its varieties, the mountain or Sargent cherry, the Yoshino cherry and the Fuji cherry.

Higan Cherry
Prunus subhirtella

The Higan cherry is familiar to us through a form with pendulous branches. The single flowers are deep pink. Above the fresh green of turf this is a most welcome sight in early spring.

'Jugatsu-zakura,' an October bloomer, does well in the equable climate of the Pacific Northwest where it flowers sporadically through the winter. Higan itself is a small bushy tree to twenty-five feet but with a low trunk virtually hidden by widespreading branches. I often think this is the most floriferous of Japanese cherries. The pale pink flowers are the largest of the group, up to one and one-half inches across. They are borne in such profusion that branches and trunk may be entirely obscured. 'Beni-higan,' the wild form, has no particular ornamental value. The pale pink single flowers are small and the tree grows to sixty feet.

The familiar 'Shidare-higan' or rosebud cherry with pendulous branches occurs in two forms. On standards the effect is an umbrella form; if branches are trained upward, a fountain effect develops up to an ultimate height of fifty feet or more. Color is variable; deep pink is popular. A double-flowered form is said to exist; this would have the advantage of prolonged bloom.

A recently introduced hybrid derived from the Higan cherry is 'Hally Jolivette,' a small tree whose semidouble fringed blooms open a few at a time over a fortnightly period. This trait is unusual among cherries, but occurs in the autumn-flowering variety of Higan cherry.

Sargent Cherry
Prunus Sargentii

'Yama-zakura,' or mountain cherry, commemorates the first director of the Arnold Arboretum, Professor Charles Sprague Sargent. It is a large tree up to sixty feet and perhaps the hardiest of oriental cherries. Clear pink flowers, one to one and three-fourths inches across, are borne in profusion. The autumn foliage is brilliant scarlet, a rare feature with oriental cherries. Narrowly conical in youth, this vigorous tree can be pruned to keep it suitable for avenue plantings.

Yoshino Cherry
Prunus yedoensis

The Yoshino cherry is a medium-sized tree with spreading branches. In bud the petals appear light pink but the single flowers open to clear white and measure slightly more than an inch across. They are faintly fragrant. The oldest known trees grow in the Imperial Botanic Gardens at Tokyo. It is this type which is planted around the Tidal Basin in Potomac Park at Washington—the type which accounts for the fine early display.

Fuji Cherry
Prunus incisa

Fuji cherry, a densely branched small tree found on the slopes of Japan's principal mountain, is popular for its profusion of white or pink blooms to three-fourths inches across. They turn red after petals fall owing to the predominance of stamens and calyx lobes that persist for a week longer. After a few warm days in April this short-stemmed cherry bursts into a cloud of bloom and is a delightful sight as a free-standing tree of some fifteen feet. It blooms consistently each year, the gray twigs hidden by the numerous flowers. Fresh green unmowed turf makes a perfect setting. The foliage, purplish upon unfolding, is finely incised at the edges. Japanese nurserymen use this species as rootstock for dwarfing many large varieties.

Purple-leaved Plum
Prunus cerasifera 'Pissardii'

The earliest of hardy cherry allies is the purple-leaved plum from southwestern Asia and the Caucasus. It is a small round-headed tree with slender twiggy branches and black scaly bark. Flowers are rosy red, small and borne before leaves develop. Recently several "improved" forms have been offered, but, as we have said, plants with foliage other than green must be used with discretion, if at all. The species is rarely found.

Two American Species

The list of cherries and their relatives should include two American species, both of which may be used to advantage in gardens. The first is the beach plum, *Prunus maritima,* a floriferous shrubby species found along the

Atlantic coastal plain and on Appalachian ridges. This species is variable in habit but blooms are uniformly spectacular and appear before leaves. Flowers are self-sterile, which means two plants are required for cross-pollination if you wish to harvest luscious bloomy plums —variable in size, season and succulence.

The second species, *Prunus serotina,* the wild black cherry, is usually considered a weed tree since it volunteers along fence row and waste places and becomes infested with tent caterpillars. What an unhappy combination of attributes. Yet mature trees, forty to sixty feet high with slender branches have superb foliage that assumes rich autumn colors. The scaly black bark is distinctive. Flowers appear with the leaves in late May and are borne in long white clusters. The tart black cherries are eagerly sought by birds.

8

Flowering Trees Galore

A GUIDE TO FORTY-ODD MORE

In this chapter you will find helpful descriptions for forty-odd other species and varieties of hardy flowering trees. More information is offered in the general chapters that follow and in the charts and lists which make up the Appendices. Trees are listed here alphabetically according to common name, with the Latin botanical name following. The common names, here and elsewhere in the book, are those that research has shown to be the most widely accepted. But if you want to be absolutely certain of a tree's identity, use the botanical name—and do not buy trees from a local nursery or an advertisement unless the botanical name for each is plainly displayed. (All trees mentioned in this book are listed alphabetically

73

by both common and botanical name, with cross references, in Appendix IV.)

Alder, white-, Japanese
Clethra barbinervis

The Japanese white-alder—more properly the Japanese clethra—is a close relative of the heath family. It is a small shrublike tree with smooth pink bark and stiff spreading branches. Erect, terminal, spikey white flower clusters are conspicuous and fragrant through most of the summer. The native shrubby species *Clethra alnifolia,* which inhabits swamps, is commonly called sweet pepper-bush or summer-sweet. In a protected location or garden, the Japanese white-alder grows twelve to fifteen feet.

Branched clusters of flowers, four to six inches high rise in rosettes among finely toothed leaves. The effect of fragrant white flowers in dark green foliage is refreshing when July days are hot.

Ash, mountain-
Sorbus

The Korean mountain-ash, *Sorbus alnifolia* (also called Atsuki-pear) has bright green alternate leaves with ten pairs of veins deeply set between lustrous wrinkled parallel ridges. This medium-sized tree looks somewhat like the birch, with ascending branches that form a rounded crown. It is a member of the rose family from eastern Asia and bears loose, few-flowered terminal clusters of white blossoms on side shoots in May. Pink berries ripen in September, a few weeks before the foliage turns a magnificent scarlet.

In cultivation the Atsuki-pear reaches a height of thirty-five to forty feet. The trunk is straight and can be pruned to a seven-foot clearance for use as a street tree. As a free-standing lawn specimen, this mountain-ash is handsome in all seasons.

The rowan tree, or European mountain-ash, *Sorbus Aucuparia,* is well known for its large clusters of bright orange fruits in August. The compound leaves, similar to but smaller than those of the ash, are borne alternately along the tip, while those of the ash are opposite.

Conspicuous in late April are the white, many-flowered clusters of blooms up to six inches across. These appear as the leaves are unfolding. Smooth gray stems hold upright the huge, slightly dome-shape clusters, but the twigs are weighted down with heavy fruits by midsummer. In silhouette, the tree is narrowly conical with smooth upright branches, a startling accent seen across a lawn in late summer. Birds relish the fleshy berries.

75

These and other species of mountain-ash inhabit cooler regions of the northern hemisphere, thriving in well-drained soils. Many grow less than twenty-five feet, and in warm regions are sometimes short-lived. Their attractive fruits, flowers and foliage amply repay their cultivation.

Beebee-tree
Evodia Daniellii

A small-to-medium-sized novelty is the so-called beebee tree, *Evodia Daniellii,* of Korea, a member of the rue or citrus family *(Rutaceae).* The Greek name *evodia* signifies pleasant odors, a characteristic of the family. In midsummer, numerous tiny, fragrant, white flowers in six-inch terminal clusters, shine like sequins through the handsome dark green foliage. Florets appear over a protracted period from mid-July on, furnishing continuous nectar for bees.

The beebee tree grows to thirty feet with spreading branches and a round-topped crown. Foliage is dark green; branches sturdy and smooth barked. Leaves are compound with tiny translucent dots along the edge that may be seen when held up to the light. Tiny black seeds like buckshot are borne in curiously shaped capsules in early autumn. Another good species, *E. hupehensis,* grows somewhat taller, to twenty-five feet.

Birch, gray (Illustration 10)
Betula populifolia

The forester tells us that the gray birch colonizes new land, dry or wet, but that as soon as taller-growing seedlings surpass it in height, its mission is accomplished. However, open grown plants survive longer than the thirty years that are commonly thought to be the age span of the gray birch. The original stem yields a number of basal suckers which form a clump and are the pride of landscape artists. White bark is also an attractive feature that is shared with few other trees.

The stem of this old-field or fire birch, as it is sometimes called, is so lithe that it bends to the weight of ice and snow. Through the winter the tree displays its long male catkins hanging from attachments near the tips of the branchlets. The female cones stand erect on slender stalks farther down the tips. Late in April the male catkins begin to loosen, and in warm weather they become yellow and are stretched to three or four inches in length. This performance takes place before the leaves unfold.

The gray birch's trunk is slender and irregularly ascending to a height of fifteen or twenty feet in cultivation.

77

Sensitive to partial shade, the trunk bends to take full advantage of light. The tree's branches are short and bushy, with innumerable dainty, triangular, pendent leaves that tremble in the slightest breeze. In autumn these leaves become pale gold, lighting up the margins of woodlands. The seeds rupture from the fruit axis in winter, dotting the snow and feeding the chickadees.

Spring-blooming bulbs are often naturalized near the white trunk of the gray birch. Or birches are interplanted among shade trees which will take longer to become established. In this way, the birch fills the empty space until the permanent tree begins to cast its shade. In age the birch looses its grace; you may have become sentimentally attached to a once-lovely tree, but there comes a time when it should be removed. This is only nature's way applied to the domestic landscape.

Birches are transplanted safely in late April to early May, with a ball of soil. Even though in nature the gray birch is not particular where it grows, in the garden it should be given a well-drained situation. Thin out the branches to balance the loss of roots in transplanting and also to display the beautiful bark.

As leaves are unfolding in early May, the birch leaf miner becomes active, feeding and laying its eggs just beneath the surface of the tender new leaves. Soon a

10. Supple, pollen-laden catkins of Gray Birch dance a jig in April's breeze while erect seed-bearing catkins await the shower of golddust at the base of unfolding leaves.

79

brown spot, caused by the feeding of the larva, appears on the leaf and enlarges rapidly until the entire leaf is discolored. Birches are able to continue developing leaves but the trees can become unsightly. Control these insects by spraying with lindane in early May, when they are feeding.

Buckthorn, woolly
Bumelia lanuginosa

Woolly or false buckthorn, a small tree, bears bunches of tiny white flowers amid lustrous leathery leaves in late summer. The chittimwood (or chittamwood) as it is sometimes called, inhabits dry rocky glades of the Middle West, growing among red-cedar, redbud, and flowering dogwood. Horizontal, somewhat tortuous branches are picturesque. This is a sturdy, slow-growing small tree, twelve to fifteen feet tall. A deep root system makes it almost insensitive to droughts. The clusters of small, fragrant, creamy white bell-shaped blooms arise in August from spurs along the spiny branches.

The foliage of chittimwood is spatulate, lustrous and leathery. It arises in rosettes from short spurlike shoots along the gray branches. The undersides of the leaves are somewhat woolly at first, but become smooth as the season progresses. In late autumn the foliage turns orange-red. Fleshy, egg-shaped black berries ripen in October.

Woolly buckthorn is well suited to difficult growing conditions. However, it is not regarded as iron-hardy in the colder sections of the northern states. Owing to its deep-rooting habit, it should be planted in small size and allowed to develop in place. It is excellent as a hedge or screen. The handsome foliage is retained into late autumn.

Catalpa, Chinese
Catalpa ovata

Catalpa was the name used by American Indians for the bignonia tree with ten-inch clusters of white tubular flowers spotted purple-brown. Since the native species are too tall or not well adapted to conditions in the North, I recommend the Chinese catalpa as a better proportioned plant for gardens. It is a hardy symmetrical tree, twenty feet tall, with coarse-textured olive-green leaves, borne three at a node. The creamy white, fragrant flowers have five lobes, the throat spotted dark purple and streaked orange inside. Bloom appears in June, earlier than on the native species; flowers are borne in terminal panicles after the large leaves have unfolded.

The fruit is a long cylindrical bean that splits at maturity to discharge great quantities of tiny winged seeds.

The catalpa is easy to grow, establishing quite readily. It is not fussy about soils, performing especially well in sandy situations. In drought, however, it does shed superfluous leaves. The shade it casts is dense but since the sturdy branches are high, turf can be grown under them.

Chestnut (Illustration 11)
Castanea

Most Americans of recent generations have no conception of either the usefulness or the beauty of the true American chestnut, *Castanea dentata*. Until World War I, it was an important member of the forests of the Appalachian Mountains from southern New England to northern Georgia. Now this great tree, with fragrant early summer flowers and delicious autumn nuts, has been virtually exterminated by the chestnut blight that attacks the bark. Attempts are being made, without much success, to find and collect blight-resistant specimens that have survived (or re-sprouted from stumps) in blight-stricken areas.

To replace the American chestnut ornamentally, the Chinese chestnut, *Castanea mollissima*, has been introduced, a species coming from a region where the blight

1. Yellowish tassels cover the Chestnut tree in early summer; beetles and flies bring pol-
n from the feathery stalks of nearby trees to the bur at the base of each tassel to produce
autumn's meaty nuts.

is less destructive. Oriental chestnuts are able to withstand attack, so we may hope to establish this foreign chestnut as a substitute.

Pendent yellow spikes borne in the axils of leaves near the tips of new shoots appear in mid-June. Since the tree spreads wide from a low-branched trunk, the floral effect suggests a splashing fountain, especially when seen with sunlight reflected from the lustrous leaves.

The chestnut grows in well-drained soil and withstands drought. To have chestnuts, two trees are required, because the flowers are not receptive to their own pollen. Allow fifty feet between trees if they are to be grown as low-branched specimens. In a chestnut grove, trees might be set at thirty-foot intervals.

Chestnut, horse-
Aesculus

Horse-chestnuts are showy in bloom, but there is strong prejudice against them because they often drop leaves and nuts, and the coarse foliage creates such dense shade that virtually no other plant will grow beneath it. While all this applies to the common horse-chestnut, *Aesculus Hippocastanum,* which has been in cultivation a long time, the relatives and hybrids need not be so stigmatized.

The double-flowering variety, *Aesculus Hippocasta-*

84

III. Pink petaled cascades of the Weeping Higan Cherry shower an evergreen landscape in late April.

num 'Baumannii' bears attractive white blooms that, happily, do not produce chestnuts. This is a large conical tree with rounded dome. The stout upsweeping branches form perfect S's, a sight best observed in winter.

Buds of the horse-chestnut are large, egg-shaped, mahogany-colored and sticky. Terminal ones, larger than those on lateral shoots, contain three pairs of leaves and a compact flower cluster that bursts open in the first warm days of May. The miniature leaves with their seven radiating leaflets are wonderfully folded—like an umbrella—and are arranged in opposite pairs underneath the scales. Inside the leaves the flower panicle appears perfectly formed, awaiting the flush of sap that stimulates it to expansion.

The ruby horse-chestnut, *Aesculus carnea* 'Briotii' (Color Plate IV) is also round-headed with bright scarlet blooms in early May. This is a hybrid between the European horse-chestnut and the red buckeye of America. It has firmer leaves and is usually able to withstand drought, and the leaves do not fall as readily in dry summers as do those of the common horse-chestnut. The flaming clusters of flowers around the well-developed leaves are an arresting sight in early spring. Try to place this tree in a situation where the visitor may come upon it unexpectedly.

A yellow-flowered species is the sweet buckeye, *Aesculus octandra,* from the southern Appalachian Mountains and plateaus, where it shares with the white basswood a position of importance. The buckeyes (as the American horse-chestnuts are called) have seed husks that are reddish and smooth, not at all prickly. The flower buds are dry, not sticky. This native buckeye is not so spectacular in bloom as the horse-chestnuts, and is tall and narrow with paler green leaves that have finely toothed margins.

Dove-tree
Davidia involucrata

Ascension Day marks the season in which the dove-tree blooms. The large white kerchiefs hang from the axils of equally large, coarse-toothed leaves. In 1899 the famed E. H. Wilson made the first of his many trips to remote China to obtain seeds of this plant discovered by Jean Pierre Armand David some three decades earlier. A few years earlier the French horticultural firm of Vilmorin-Andrieux et Cie. introduced a variant of the dove-tree from less remote China.

The principal attraction is its novelty, and few trees have so excited the horticultural world. In the first week of May, when only early leafage is expanding, this symmetrical tree unfurls huge petal-like bracts high in the crown and shielded among large leaves. Patience is required, however, in bringing a dove-tree to the flowering stage—some twenty years approximately. Once in bloom it is conspicuous for a fortnight or more, depending upon weather.

Belonging to the same family as the native sour gum or tupelo, the dove-tree bears small heads of tiny flowers between a pair of paper-thin heart-shaped bracts. Unlike the rugged sour gum, this Asiatic tree requires protection in severe cold winters. Planting a dove-tree north or east of an evergreen tree or screen offers ideal shelter as well as display. In August the green fruits on long stalks become the size of olives.

Ehretia, Heliotrope
Ehretia thyrsiflora

The only hardy treelike member of the borage family that includes the herbaceous perennial Virginia bluebells, is the heliotrope ehretia of eastern Asia, a narrow upright tree to thirty feet with irregular spreading branches. Tiny white flowers in erect three- to eight-inch terminal clusters appear in June. Small olive-green berries clustered above the drooping leaves are prominent in summer. In August the fruits turn orange and finally ripen brownish black.

87

The bark of this straight-stemmed, easily established tree resembles that of the ash. Although ehretias grow vigorously in the South, they develop more slowly in the North.

Empress-tree (Illustrations 1 and 2, pages 13 and 25)
Paulownia tomentosa

Before the soft hairy leaves unfold in May the empress-tree or royal paulownia bursts into bloom. Lavender catalpa-like flowers are borne on erect branched panicles at the ends of the branches. In excessively cold winters the vulnerable brown woolly flower buds may be killed, with consequent loss of flowers the next spring. Heavy bloom one season and prolific development of seed will also reduce the development of new flower buds. Fruit capsule and flower bud of the Empress tree are sometimes confused. An easy way to distinguish them is to open up a structure. Seeds appear as tiny winged discs, whereas the flower bud is a pale mass of vegetable matter whose composition is only revealed under lens or microscope.

The empress-tree, growing to fifty feet or more, is coarse foliaged, resembling the catalpa except for the hairy leaves in pairs. Catalpa leaves are smooth and in threes. Stump sprouts, which develop when roots are left after the tree is felled, often bear leaves the size of elephant ears. The species is from southeastern Asia, but has become naturalized throughout the South and as far north as New Jersey and Long Island, where it grows at the edge of woodland as well as in home plantings.

Epaulette-tree (Illustrations 12 and 13)
Pterostyrax hispida

After the large leaves have expanded in early June, the epaulette-tree reveals clusters of delicate, fringed white flowers resembling military shoulder ornaments, and so the common name. The fragrant blossoms are arranged in tiers from hanging clusters, five to ten inches long, at the ends of short lateral branchlets. Florets have five narrow petals which produce the fringed effect. In August fuzzy fruits hang in slender chains through the open canopy of foliage and remain decorative after the leaves fall.

The epaulette-tree grows to thirty feet or more with slender spreading branches. As in the related snowbells and silverbells, the second-year branchlets show fibrous shreds along the bark. A background of needled evergreens sets off the daintiness of this Asiatic relative of the genus *Styrax*.

12. Resemblance of its flowers to epaulettes provides this Japanese tree with its com
mon name, Epaulette-tree; the ranks of white tassels hanging among pale green leave
readily suggest legions of military heroes on parade.

13. After its leaves have fallen in October, the Epaulette-tree's hairy fruits extend the garden season.

FLOWERING TREES

Franklin-tree
Franklinia alatamaha

The rarest of American flowering trees, the Franklin-tree, was discovered about 1790 by William Bartram of Pennsylvania on a plant hunt along the banks of the Altamaha River of Georgia. He named it in honor of Benjamin Franklin. The original colony of trees was destroyed and the species has not since been seen in the wild. The plants we now grow in our gardens have all been derived from those that Bartram propagated in his nursery at Kingsessing, then a village on the west bank of the Schuylkill River near Philadelphia.

From early August until frost, white cup-shaped flowers unfold a few at a time among the leaves near the tips of the current year's shoots. The Franklin-tree, often shrublike, with smooth ascending branches, makes narrow compact growth fifteen to twenty feet high in well-drained acid soil. Twigs are green, becoming dark gray with narrow white lines along the slender branches. Like the flowering dogwood and sassafras, the Franklin-tree makes a wavy branch since the twig is lengthened by a lateral bud.

Lustrous spatulate leaves, eight inches long, provide a perfect setting for the pure white-petaled blooms, three

92

inches across and close to the axils of the leaves. In autumn these turn brilliant red. In the North the Franklin-tree seldom sets fruit. To get a tree-like form, train the plant to a single stem while it is still young.

Fringe-tree, white
Chionanthus virginicus

In June when the weather is warm and settled, the white fringe-tree reveals its floral beauty. Its scientific name is derived from the Greek *chion,* snow, and *anthos,* flower. The four petals are pure white, narrow, and flaring. They hang in loose clusters beneath the unfolding leaves. The effect is enchanting—soft white against pale green. Male flowers, borne on separate plants from those of the berry-producing female flowers, are slightly larger and appear more profusely.

The native white fringe-tree, growing to twenty feet, is shrublike with a short trunk and ascending branches that form a rounded crown. The leaves, three to eight inches long, are dark green when mature, of firm texture and with smooth margins. They are opposite on the twig and in autumn turn bright yellow. This tree grows naturally in low moist places, but it also thrives in upland gardens having normal moisture and fertility.

The Oriental fringe-tree, *C. retusus,* with later flower

93

clusters borne at the tips of the twigs, has shorter, broader petals. This species is somewhat lower in stature, although trunk and crown are better developed than in the American species. Leaves are smaller, from one to four inches long, usually with a slightly notched tip. In bloom this tree is a veritable snow storm, with erect four-inch clusters of flowers covering the leafy branches.

Golden-chain, Waterer's (Color Plate V)
Laburnum Watereri

The golden-chain tree makes a beautiful picture when clusters of yellow flowers hang from the branches. Except for color, the pendent stalks of flowers suggest wisteria. This tree, with tapered form, is the laburnum of Europe. It blooms in mid-May as the trifoliolate leaves unfold. Planted next to lavender wisteria, blooming at the same time, it is a lovely sight.

Waterer's golden-chain tree is derived from two southern European species, the common laburnum of alpine foothills and the so-called Scotch laburnum of the Alps. *Laburnum Watereri* and *L. Vossii* appear to be identical. The golden-chain tree grows to twenty feet or so and develops a low branching trunk. The principal branches are upright while the secondary ones are arching. The smooth bark is greenish brown marked with horizontal

94

lenticels like those on a cherry tree. Nodding flower clusters nearly a foot long hang from the tips of branchlets, making a conspicuous display. The dry, tan bean pods, which remain on the branches until winter, are hardly attractive, except perhaps in dried arrangements.

A moist alkaline soil and light shade are preferred; full sun in summer is likely to scorch leaves. The goldenchain does not succeed in regions of mild winters except along the coast of Maine and similar areas. For recurring bloom and to keep the tree in pleasing proportion, head back the long shoots in midsummer. One striking use of this charming tree is as an espalier against a northeast wall.

Goldenrain-tree (Illustration 14)
Koelreuteria paniculata

The goldenrain-tree or varnish tree commemorates Professor Joseph G. Koelreuter of Karlsruhe, Germany, a plant hybridizer of two centuries ago. *Koelreuteria paniculata* is a dense, medium-sized, round-headed tree bearing foot-long terminal clusters of bright yellow flowers in July.

Leaves are pinnately compound with seven to fifteen leaflets, each irregularly toothed or lobed. The dull green leaf surface provides a soft texture. Branchlets are

95

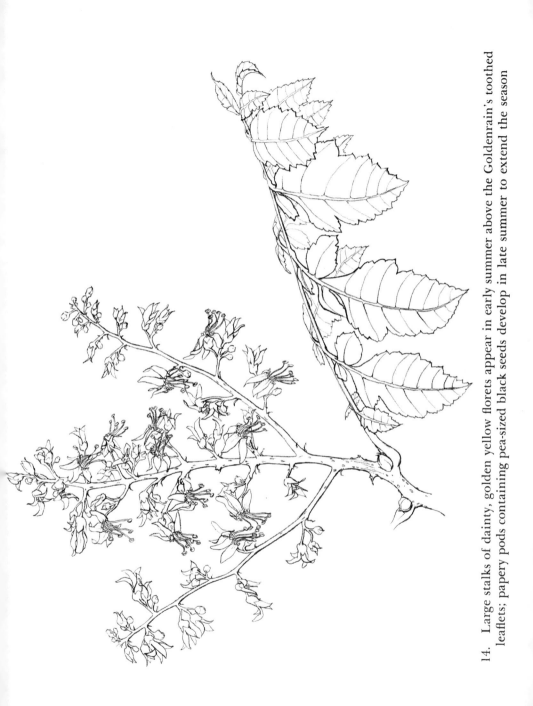

14. Large stalks of dainty, golden yellow florets appear in early summer above the Goldenrain's toothed leaflets; papery pods containing pea-sized black seeds develop in late summer to extend the season

thick and curiously crooked, giving the tree a rugged look. The stout, scaly barked trunk is further convoluted and sometimes inclined, accentuating the illusion of sturdiness. And illusion it is, since the roots are frequently unable to hold up the heavy canopy of foliage unless the planting site is protected and out of strong wind.

Hawthorn, Washington
Crataegus Phaenopyrum

From the very long list of hawthorn species, I choose as my favorite the native species commonly grown in Washington, D.C., namely the Washington thorn, *Crataegus Phaenopyrum* (or *C. cordata*). True, it has thorns, but it does not lose its foliage in midseason as the English hawthorn *(C. oxyacanthoides)* sometimes does (Illustration 15). The combined display of autumn foliage and scarlet-orange berries is unexcelled and the berries often remain until winter. They are striking against an evergreen background.

The Washington thorn is a small tree, about twenty feet tall, with a straight trunk and slender, zigzag branches that form a rounded crown. The fine, triangular foliage resembles that of the gray birch, up to three and one-half inches long, pale green and glossy. Con-

15.   Doubled scarlet petals prolong the English Hawthorn's velvety floral display in early May; occasional thorns hide beneath the refined foliage but haws
seldom form on this highly bred flowering tree.

cealed by the leaves are long thorns—not a drawback, however, if the lower branches are removed. The tree makes a handsome free-standing specimen or several, informally grouped, may be used as a screen or accent.

The principal difficulty with hawthorns, as with other members of the apple or rose family, is their susceptibility to fire blight and cedar-apple rust, both of which disfigure foliage and may even kill a tree. They can be controlled (see cultural sections at end of book) by careful pruning and preventive spraying.

Idesia polycarpa

Idesia does not have a common name, and it is rarely seen in northern gardens. The large heart-shaped leaves, silvery underneath, hang from slightly up-turned whorls of branches. Seen below the foliage are loose ten-inch clusters of fragrant greenish white flowers borne at the tips of short shoots in May. As with holly, the sexes occur on different trees. To obtain red berries, it is necessary to have a pollen-bearing or male tree near a female tree.

The leaves, five to ten inches long, are large, and the stout trunk supports a broad crown to form a coarse-textured tree. Of doubtful adaptation in colder sections of the North, *Idesia* grows rapidly—to thirty feet—where it

99

is hardy. This tree belongs to the subtropical family, *Flacourtiaceae,* whose members yield medicinal oils.

Lilac, tree-, Japanese
Syringa amurensis var. *japonica*

The faint perfume of the huge creamy panicles of the Japanese tree-lilac attracts honey-bees and delights the gardener's nose in early June, although the fragrance does suggest privet, the lilac and privet being members of the olive family. The conspicuous flower clusters rise in pairs at the tips of the shoots and are about twelve inches long. Foliage is fully expanded at the time of bloom. The green tapering leaves are egg-shaped, two to six inches long and borne opposite. The olive-brown cherrylike bark with pale yellowish dots is attractive too. Identification as a lilac is established by the opposite leaves and the panicle of tiny, four-petaled flowers which in autumn become dry capsuled fruits.

The tree-lilac is less than twenty feet tall with a rounded crown and ascending branches. The Japanese variety, a good plant, is preferred to the species. The species comes from the Amur region of Manchuria and responds to springlike weather in late winter by swelling its buds and sometimes unfolding a few leaves.

The Peking lilac, *Syringa pekinensis,* blooms later with

less foliage and peeling rather red bark. This species from the ancient Chinese capitol city of Peking, was introduced to this country some eighty years ago by the Arnold Arboretum in Jamaica Plain, Massachusetts, near Boston.

What a charming small flowering tree this is, growing to less than twenty feet with a loose open form and rounded crown. The terminal clusters of fragrant, creamy, mid-June flowers are also open and up to six inches long. This tree belongs in the intimate garden where its many charming attributes may be observed at close range.

Linden (Illustration 16)
Tilia

June is incomplete without the linden. So prodigious is its crop of sweet-smelling flowers that the linden is a tree that may be "heard" in bloom—bees by the hive-full are irresistibly lured to it. Several species and hybrids extend the linden season over a whole month. The first flowers to open are those of the European, so-called large-leaved, linden, *Tilia platyphyllos.* Compared with other Old World lindens, foliage is large perhaps, but the American linden or basswood *(Tilia americana)* of northern forests also frequently bears larger leaves.

101

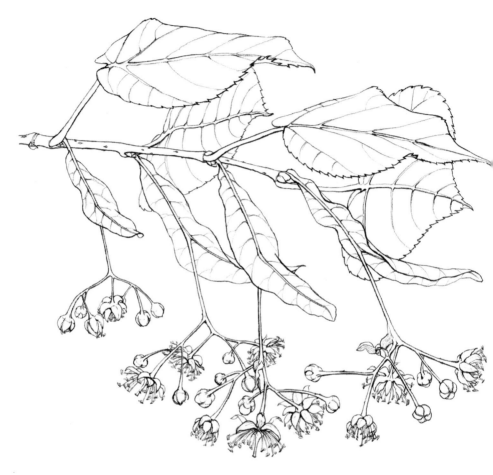

16.   Sweet fragrance in June tells of the Linden's blossoming; creamy yellow flowers, in clusters of seven or more, hang on winged stalks amid glossy, dark green, heart-shaped leaves.

In Europe, especially, lindens are also known as limes. These limes (not to be confused with citrus limes) are planted along avenues, in parks, and elsewhere throughout Europe. Round-headed, with arching, often pendent branches, they are densely covered with small, often shiny, dark green, heart-shaped leaves. With age the bark becomes furrowed, and if damaged shoots arise from the injured area.

The flowers hang from long winged stalks that arise in the axils of the leaves. In clusters not unlike the pawnbroker's emblem, they open creamy fragrant blooms and also attract the bee.

Other lindens include the Crimean, *Tilia euchlora,* with fine-toothed glossy leaves; the littleleaf European, *T. cordata,* with small leaves and the latest blooms; the silver, *T. tomentosa,* with a broad conical outline and leaves silvery on the reverse; the pendent silver, *T. petiolaris,* similar to it but with pendulous branches, and the basswood, *T. americana,* a massive tree with large leaves and reddish, ridged bark. Linden leaves alternate on the branchlets. Buds are plump, reddish and of equal size— there is no larger terminal one at the end of the twig.

Locust, black
Robinia Pseudoacacia

Pendent clusters of white flowers are a striking feature of the black locust in June—especially when seen in silhouette against the deep blue sky. A pervading fragrance arises from the pea-shaped blooms which appear among the fresh leaves. The flower clusters often measure six inches in length.

The black locust, sometimes called false acacia, has bluish green foliage of refined texture, providing an ideal background for the tree's own flowers and for the garden as a whole. Leaves, consisting of oppositely arranged small oval leaflets tipped with tiny bristles, vary from four to twelve inches in length. Shade cast by the compound leaves is filmy, creating open patterns across lawns and allowing turf to thrive right up to the base of the trunk. The black locust is among the last deciduous trees to shed leaves in autumn.

Ruggedness characterizes the deeply furrowed gray bark with its shaggy interlacing ridges. The bare trunk, erect but crooked, grows to a height of thirty or forty feet, emphasizing the tree's look of sturdiness and dependability even in the face of adverse conditions. The yellowish brown wood is hard and heavy—ask anyone who has worked it with a handsaw.

The tree is easy to establish. In fact, it was formerly much planted in groves in the northern coastal plain beyond its natural range and is now an escape or wild plant in New York and southern New England. As the sassafras, sumac and the tree of heaven *(Ailanthus)*, the black locust spreads by root suckers, and it also has an extensive root system. This is a disadvantage on small properties, but is beneficial for the stabilization of sandy soils and steep banks. The tree is a legume, and its noduled roots enrich the soil with nitrogen-bearing bacteria.

Sometimes leaf-mining insects cause foliage to turn unsightly brown in June. These can be controlled by spraying the new foliage with malathion according to directions on the package. Twig-boring insects sometimes invade young shoots, causing swelling or galls. Infested branches are weakened so that winter wind and storm bring them down. Since attacks rate as little more than a nuisance, pruning is the easiest control. The current season's branchlets also are set with sharp thorns on either side of the leaf. In winter these spines fall, to be replaced the following summer if shoots grow vigorously.

FLOWERING TREES

Maackia

The maackia does not have a common name and is not well known. Yet the so-called Chinese maackia, growing fifty to sixty feet, is a delightful summer-blooming tree. A member of the pea family, it has erect clusters of creamy flowers in mid-July; they are borne conspicuously at the tips of branches, against a background of olive-green foliage. Five or six thickly clustered upright racemes, five to eight inches tall and composed of small blooms that resemble sweet peas, make up the floral display. This hardy tree grows fifty to sixty feet high.

Several species are found in eastern Asia. All, including the forty-foot *Maackia amurensis,* are hardy enough for our northern areas. However, as with other leguminous plants that bear flowers at the tips of the branches, maackias sometimes fail to bloom consistently. The trees have a neat upright branching habit. Reddish brown bark looks soft and smooth as silk.

Olive, Russian-
Elaeagnus angustifolia

The Russian-olive or oleaster, also called Trebizond date, is an excellent small-flowering tree for the seashore since it can endure strong winds and salt spray. But a shore environment is a challenge. Unless humus is added to the sandy soil to retain moisture, rainfall and hose watering quickly pass beyond the roots and abundant bright sunshine and constant breezes create stress conditions by increasing the need for water. Even the seashore gardener often must also set up wind screens and apply soil mulches. The list of woody plants that can tolerate seashore situations is restricted. Russian-olive, growing up to twenty feet or so, is one such tree.

Russian-olive is a member of the Oleaster family and not a true olive. It blooms in June. The yellow, slightly fragrant but inconspicuous flowers are borne singly, or in clusters of two's and three's in the axils of the silvery scaled leaves. Small silvery yellow berries resembling olives ripen in early autumn. The scientific name, *Elaeagnus,* is derived from the Greek *elaia,* olive, and *agnos,* the classical name for the chaste-tree.

Pear, Callery (Illustration 17)
Pyrus Calleryana

From Europe and from Asia come about twenty species of pears. Many have been grown for centuries for their luscious fruit. Their bane is fireblight, a fungus disease that withers branches. Commercial growers brought from China the Callery pear, *Pyrus Calleryana,*

107

17. The Pear, with its glistening white flowers in terminal clusters against April's azure sky, is a springtime favorite; glossy green leaves appear as the blossoms fade.

that resists attack by the fire-blight fungus. They use it as rootstock, grafting choice varieties onto it in the hope that these too may become resistant. As so often happens, the importation of the Callery pear has brought a second benefit of importance to home gardeners. The tree developed so handsomely and performed so well in introduction gardens and nurseries that it gained renown as an ornamental. One recent Callery pear selection introduced by the United States Department of Agriculture is called 'Bradford.'

A symmetrical, medium-sized tree, twenty-five or thirty feet tall, it bears white flowers slightly in advance of the leaves, and has a deep red-purple foliage color late in autumn. Sharp thorns rise on spur shoots, but this objectionable feature can be overcome simply by the removal of lower branches.

The pungent-smelling flowers are best seen as a mass of white against a blue mid-April sky. In contrast to crab-apples, flowers of the Callery pear are stiff and erect, the anthers red, not yellow, as in most crabapples. The small round pears are brown with a dotted skin. The five calyx lobes at the blossom end of the fruit are spreading, whereas in apples these appendages are closed.

Photinia villosa

Another handsome tree without a common name, photinia grows to about fifteen feet with a short trunk and spreading branches. About forty species of *Photinia,* members of the rose family, are found in southern and eastern Asia. One is sometimes called the Christmasberry because of its bright-red hawlike berries. A thirty to forty-foot species, *P. serrulata,* is handsome and often evergreen but not too hardy; *P. villosa* is perhaps the hardiest of the group. The flaming autumn foliage comes to its peak after other plants have shed their leaves. Twiggy branches offer ideal nesting sites for birds.

White flowers in clusters up to two inches across arise terminally on short lateral shoots in mid-May or June. The fine toothed leaves, up to three and one-fourth inches long, are broader above the middle and are attached to the twig by exceedingly short stalks. This creates a dense mass of foliage.

Raisin-tree
Hovenia dulcis

The raisin-tree of China bears fragrant greenish flowers in upright, three-to-four inch clusters; they ripen into club-shaped, edible red fruits. This is not the raisin of commerce, actually a dried grape, but belongs instead to the buckthorn family *(Rhamnaceae)*, a group known for cathartic properties as well as its tasty fruits. A relative, the jujube *(Zizyphus)*, also from China, is raised for its edible datelike fruits.

Bees are attracted to the raisin-tree's sweet-smelling early summer flowers. A round-headed tree to thirty feet, the raisin-tree has large leaves like those of the dove-tree. The leaves occur alternately along slender graceful branchlets.

Redbud (Illustration 18)
Cercis canadensis

The redbud or Judas tree, with knots of rose-pink blooms along arching black-barked branches, is among the showiest of small native trees. It blooms in late April, while the leaves are still to come. The early-swelling buds are decorative for several days before they open. On that account the tree is best displayed against a background of native red cedar or other needled evergreen. The blooms arise in clusters from buds marking the position of last year's leaves. Curiously, some flower clusters are also borne along older branches and even on the trunk. Actually the bloom is produced on tiny spurs or short

111

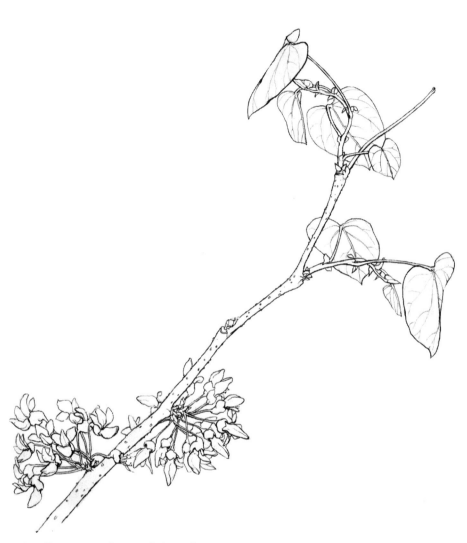

18.   Bouquets of rosy pink buds decorate the gray stems of the Redbud; when these fade, coppery, heart-shaped leaves provide a secondary display; flowers are borne on short shoots although they seem to come from the stem.

112

shoots that were developed when the branch bore leaves at that position.

Growing to less than twenty feet, the redbud forms a rounded crown with slender arching branches. Shiny heart-shaped leaves up to four inches across and smooth along the edges, rise alternately along the branchlets with a stalk swollen at either end.

Flat, beanlike pods attain full size, about three inches long, by late May. These are bright rose at first but become dry and brown by midsummer and remain on the branches until winter. In autumn the foliage turns clear yellow, creating a sunny effect against the darkness of evergreens.

The redbud grows in bottom lands, along streams and in limestone glades. Native to the southeastern United States and southern Ontario, it grows best in the South. The tree is found in company with service-berry and flowering dogwoods, and the rose-pink blooms harmonize with the clean whites of such flowering neighbors and the greens of conifers. A white-flowering form, variety *alba,* is available and well worth consideration.

Scholar-tree, Chinese (Illustration 19)
Sophora japonica

Late in July, when flowering trees are both rare and welcome, the Chinese scholar-tree opens creamy yellow flowers borne at the tips of the branches. No matter how hot and dry the season, the Chinese scholar, also called Japanese pagoda tree, is a refreshing sight. The leaves, of fine texture, retain their springtime freshness regardless of the midseason condition of the lawn and the foliage is sufficiently open to permit grass to grow, yet the shade offers full protection from strong summer sunshine.

The nectar-rich, pea-shaped blooms, in loose, many-flowered clusters at the ends of the current season's green twigs, appear a few at a time for a period of two to three weeks. Petals falling to the ground look like a shower of gold. Pale green seed pods are distinctive since they are constricted between the seeds, giving the appearance of a string of beads.

A round-headed tree to fifty feet, the Chinese scholar-tree has a short trunk. It is planted in its native China and Korea as well as in Europe as a street tree. Here, nurserymen are developing a form with a seven-foot trunk so that the species may be used along modern av-

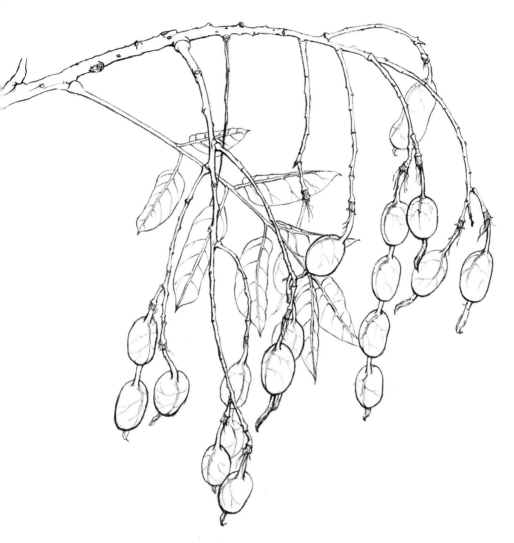

19. Emerald necklaces tip the branches of the Chinese Scholar-tree in autumn, following a midsummer floral display of green and gold; flowers are numerous but tiny, remaining in bloom over a prolonged period in the summer.

115

enues where clearance in excess of twelve feet is required. Only the dropping of the soft fruits onto sidewalks in November constitutes a possible drawback to the adoption of the Chinese scholar tree as an ideal street tree.

The glossy bright green leaves remain attractive into autumn. In some seasons they turn yellow before they fall, but usually they stay green. Warm weather continuing into late autumn is a disadvantage to the scholar-tree since it may be unable to ripen tip growth, which is then likely to be killed back by frosts. Delay in leaf expansion the next spring is a result of this, and the long-term consequence may be failure to bloom.

Service-berry (Illustration 20)
Amelanchier laevis

The first native flowering tree in the North to bloom is the Allegheny or smooth service-berry, also called shadblow, shadbush or June-berry, an understory tree in Eastern woodlands. Sharp-pointed buds on slender gray branchlets unfold to reveal graceful nodding clusters of white flowers, a most delicate breath of spring. Ascending, smooth-barked branches form an oval crown. When the shadbush blooms, it looks like a low-lying fleecy cloud or a mist. Unfolding leaves are rose-colored. As the flower petals fall, the leaves become fully expanded and

116

IV.   Bright scarlet candles light the bold dark green foliage of Ruby Horse-chest-
       nut in early May.

20. In early springtime, aggregates of glistening white petals surmount the Service-berry's slender upsweeping stems. Leaves are rosy-colored as they unfold and transform to green when fully expanded.

117

are pale green. In June and July sweet, juicy, bluish-purple berries ripen to delight robins and other song-birds.

The Allegheny service-berry grows to fifteen or twenty feet. It needs water in dry spells and mulch helps to keep the soil moist. When the service-berry is trained to a single stem it develops into an oval-shaped small tree of great charm. Ferns and wild flowers may be naturalized beneath it.

Silk-tree
Albizia Julibrissin var. rosea

Even in temperate latitudes the hardy silk-tree seems luxuriantly tropical, with scented pink powderpuffs of bloom appearing all summer among the delicate pale green leaves. Flat-topped with spreading gray-hued branches, it grows thirty to forty feet tall in the South. In the North it remains low branching, scarcely exceeding twenty feet in height and somewhat more in spread. This pink-flowered tree thrives in sites of good drainage —both soil and air—and makes rapid growth. The tracery of shadow created by the myriad tiny leaflets permits the growth of lawns and flowers that do not require full sun. If the lower branches are pruned high enough, chairs may be placed under the filtered shade.

The delicate, fragrant blooms which begin to appear in late June, consist of compact heads of tiny soft brush-like pink filaments without petals. This type of flower differs from the butterfly pattern common among legumes. The fruits, however, are flat greenish pods that contain a few brown beans, characteristic of this family.

On the debit side the mimosa webworm attacks this species, forming threadlike tents over portions of the branches. The foliage inside the tents gets brown and unsightly. A mixture of DDT and kerosene squirted from a trigger-pressured oil can or pressure sprayer gives control. Another debit for northern gardeners: a severe winter may damage (or even kill) a tree in an exposed site.

Silverbell (Illustrations 21 and 22)
Halesia

Last year's shoots are strung with glistening white bell-shaped blooms, up to one and one-half inches in length, before the silverbell opens its leaves in early May. Each cluster is composed of three or four flowers and these extend for a foot or so along the sweeping branches. Two species are important, *Halesia carolina,* or *H. tetraptera,* the Carolina silverbell, an understory tree of southeastern forests, and *H. monticola,* the mountain silverbell,

119

21. Festoons of dainty white bells bring gaiety to landscape when the Silver-bell blooms in early spring; the fallen petals leave a sword-like style that hardens into a point on the winged fruit.

120

22. Clusters of green fruits ribbed with four wings hang from shreddy second-year branches of the Silverbell.

a canopy tree common in the southern Appalachian forests of the Great Smoky Mountains.

The Carolina silverbell grows fifteen to twenty feet and develops a single stem if pruned and trained at an early age. The large green leaves unfold after the flower petals fall. Leaves are alternate along the branchlets. In autumn they turn yellow, provided the growing season is prolonged. The brown winged fruits, one and one-half inches long, are decorative pendants along the sweeping branches.

The mountain silverbell in nature is a tall and round-topped tree. In cultivation, it has a conical silhouette and grows to forty feet. The trunk attains a girth of ten or twelve inches and is covered with thick bark. The pale rose-flowered form, *H. monticola* 'Rosea,' is preferred for gardens. The flowers, two to five in a cluster, hang on one-inch stems, the pink petals extend up for another inch.

Smoke-tree (Illustration 23)
Cotinus Coggygria

The bright, hot days of July bring on the bloom of the smoke-tree, also called Venetian sumac. It decorates gardens at the same time that the native sumacs brighten roadsides. Smoke-tree takes its name from the feathery

23. A few seeds are enough to hold the feathery clouds hovering above the shrub-like Smoke-tree throughout the summer.

123

flower or fruiting clusters that hover like fog on the branches throughout the summer. The buff-colored "smoke" consists of feathered stalks that remain after most of the miniature flowers have fallen. Only a few flowers need receive pollen in order to allow the tiny berries to develop and the filmy cluster to persist.

Smoke-tree is sometimes listed under the botanical name *Rhus Cotinus* (for it is related to the sumacs and other members of the genus *Rhus*). It is a small shrub-like tree with large rounded leaves borne on long stalks. The foliage in summer is screened by the "smoke," but in autumn the leaves take on deep reddish shades before falling. The plant is large for a shrub and small for a tree. It looks best as a free-standing specimen, although it is handsome in front of a Cape Cod cottage.

Although not related botanically, the crape-myrtle is like the smoke-tree in its shrub/tree or tree/shrub characteristic. Botanically *Lagerstroemia indica,* it belongs to the family that includes the herbaceous perennial *Lythrum*. Where it is hardy, crape-myrtle grows to about twenty feet, and produces a spectacular crop of pink, red or white flower clusters almost all summer. However, where winters go to zero *L. indica* is not likely to survive (or it may be killed to the ground every winter and never have a chance to achieve treelike proportions). If planted in a sheltered spot, it may do well—as a number of happy gardeners in the New York area will attest.

Snowbell (Illustration 24)
Styrax

A profusion of bells marks the blooming of the Japanese snowbell or storax, *Styrax japonica,* in late May. This flowering tree waits until its finely toothed leaves are expanded before opening its delicate pendent blooms, which are best seen from beneath. The branches develop from a short trunk to form a spreading horizontal tree, twelve to fifteen feet tall. The leaves, broadly elliptic, up to three inches long, with tapering tip and base, have a metallic green luster.

The white flowers, borne in clusters of five or six, arise at the tip of twiggy lateral shoots along the slender branches. Each blossom, about three-fourths of an inch across, consists of five flaring petals and a bundle of gold-tipped stamens with a single white projecting style. In autumn, gray berries on slender one-inch stalks decorate the bare branchlets.

Japanese snowbell grows readily from seed. Since the root system is delicate, care is required in transplanting. Take a solid ball of soil lest the roots be disturbed and

125

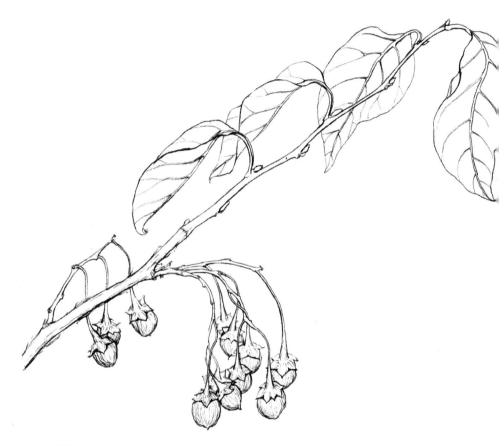

24. Silky, green, hard-shelled fruits hang in clusters among metallic green foliage Japan's Snowbell; seeds sprout readily but seedlings are not easily transplant

the plant die. The tree is best moved in the seedling stage and under four feet.

A larger, coarse-leaved tree is the fragrant snowbell *Styrax Obassia*, also from Japan. Long terminal racemes of thirty or more white flowers appear a few days after those of the other Japanese species. This tree is broadly conical, about twenty feet tall, with ascending branches. The leaves, from three to eight inches long, are almost round. Flower clusters, nearly eight inches long, rise from the tips of short branches and project beyond the pale green leaves for a fine display. Plant the fragrant storax in front of needled evergreens for effective contrast.

Sourwood
Oxydendrum arboreum

Sorrel-tree or sourwood is an understory tree of the southern Appalachian forests. Thriving in acid soils, it grows symmetrically to twenty to thirty feet with flaring pendent racemes of white flowers, like those of lily-of-the-valley. It is delightful in summer and autumn.

The sourwood should be planted in a sunny site with loose, well-drained, acid soil. A mulch helps to insure a cool moist condition.

The thick bark, checkered like alligator hide, shows

127

orange tissue between the plates. Branches ascend in whorls from the straight trunk. Lustrous peachlike leaves, six to eight inches long, are pale green and fine toothed. In midsummer, when few trees are in bloom, the sourwood is welcome, with its graceful sweep of flowers so attractive to bees. In October the leaves turn scarlet but stay pale beneath. The sorrel-tree combines memorably with soft-textured evergreens such as white pine or hemlock.

Stewartia (Illustration 25)

Members of the genus *Stewartia* (or *Stuartia*)—there is no widely popular common name—bear fringed, white, solitary cup-shaped blooms, two and one-half to four inches across. The flowers start to appear in late June, continuing for a month. Branches ascend from smooth stems, forming small round-headed trees less than twenty feet tall. Taper-tipped oval leaves, up to three and one-half inches long and sparsely toothed along the edges, form a dense canopy. Glimpses of reddish brown bark, mottled by flaky patches, may be caught through the foliage. Stewartias need rich moist loam, somewhat acid.

Earliest to bloom is the Korean stewartia, *S. koreana*. Its fringe-petaled flowers frequently measure four inches across. They consist of five to eight cup-shaped petals

25. The Mountain Stewartia, America's prized member of the tea family, displays fringed white petals surrounding purple stalked anthers. Luxurious foliage provides a handsome setting for the single blooms.

attached to a whorl of incurved yellow stamens. After pollination takes place, this whole envelope falls in one piece, littering the ground. The bark of the Korean stewartia is variously pink, green and brown, and bears a striking resemblance to that of the lacebark pine.

The Japanese stewartia's scientific name, *S. Pseudo-Camellia,* suggests its relationship to the familiar camellia, also a member of the tea family. This species blooms later and is smaller in flower size than the Korean stewartia, and grows somewhat taller and narrower in silhouette. The leaves are smaller and the bark is a deeper pink. In autumn the leaves turn a purplish color.

The notably hardier American mountain stewartia, known to some as mountain camellia *(S. ovata),* is shorter in stature, usually not over fifteen feet tall, and later blooming. The variety *S. ovata* variety *grandiflora* has larger and more handsome flowers, up to four inches across.

Tree of Heaven (Illustration 26)
Ailanthus altissima

Maligned and outcast, the tree of heaven from China is a colonizer of waste places, such as sterile bankings; it thrives in sooty atmospheres and it invades forest clearings. Seeds of this adaptable tree were sent in 1751 to Bernard de Jussieu at Paris and to Philip Miller at Chel-

26. Tree of Heaven's twisted papery winged seeds decorate the stout branches during early winter; the wind detaches each seed to carry it far afield.

131

sea by Father Pierre d'Incarville, a Jesuit missionary-botanist stationed at Peking. The species was introduced to America in 1784. It has been widely planted and has since escaped to roadsides, vacant lots, railroad embankments, basement areaways and other unlikely sites.

Apparently immune to attacks of insects or disease, the tree of heaven is indifferent to atmospheric pollution and abusive treatment. It is more productive even on poor sites than poplar or willow. The wood compares favorably with oak for firewood and is useful in millwork.

Why should such an adaptable plant be spurned by gardeners? Some scorn it for the strong scent of its male flowers, but they are usually oblivious to it during the balance of the year. Because its seedlings spring up in the unlikeliest places, some curse its fecundity. Still others object to its coarse texture, its thick stalks and long compound leaves.

The brief in its favor is simply this: it is able to sprout and grow in sites where other species cannot survive. It is able to bloom and to set seed. It withstands drought, poor soil, smoke. This species thrives in downtown sites where space is at a premium and other species are unable to exist.

Eleven or more glossy tapering leaflets, two to six

inches long, arranged in pairs along a graceful curved stalk up to three feet in length make the tree of heaven foliage appear coarse. The leaves radiate from the stout branches in large rosettes. At their center a large cluster of tiny greenish flowers appears in June. The sexes arise on separate trees, and the pollen-bearing flowers have a carrion odor.

In August the wings of the fruit become bright red or yellow, contrasting handsomely with the lustrous dark green foliage, appearing as flowers nestled in the huge rosettes. The leaves begin to fall early in October leaving bunches of beautifully twisted straw-colored seeds as an added display for the late autumn. Wintry winds detach and disperse the winged seeds to out-of-the-way and seemingly hostile places where they soon sprout unnoticed.

The tree of heaven sometimes grows to considerable heights, but in sites where fertility is low and drainage is poor it forms a low domed top at about forty feet. The many ascending branches make a pleasing silhouette along the winter skyline. Twigs are stout and coarse with large leaf scars and buds. They are distinguished by a smooth bark, clear sap, a rank odor when crushed, and solid tan pith.

Tulip-tree (Color Plate VI, Illustration 27)
Liriodendron Tulipifera

Flowering at about the same time as the magnolia is the related tulip-tree, *Liriodendron Tulipifera,* with its tall straight trunk and distinctive leaves. The tuliplike flowers are yellowish with a brown spot. The blossoms are attractive close up, but not conspicuous amid the mass of bright green foliage. However, the tan "cones" show to advantage against the clear autumn or winter sky. The yellow leaves caught in October breezes present a truly gay sight. When the tulip-tree or yellow poplar (a suggestive but misleading name) loses leaves during the summer, it is an indication that drought is severe.

Two species of *Liriodendron,* literally lily-tree, are extant, one each in the Old and New Worlds. In geological times the tulip-tree had an extensive range. Today it is confined to the moist fertile soils of the temperate zone. The buds, resembling a duck's bill, consist of a pair of stipules which, when opened, reveal the neatly folded leaf. The leaves are curiously fashioned at the tip. Upon close examination, you will find that the midvein of each leaf blade ends in a short point, the leaf extending beyond in prominent lateral lobes.

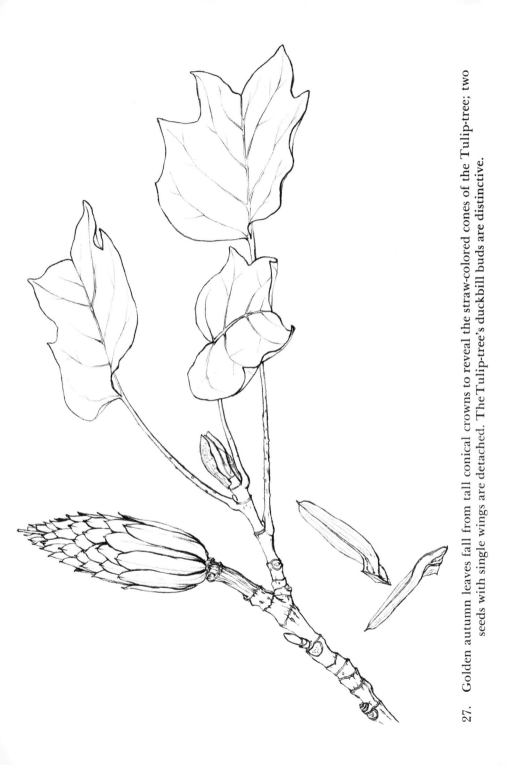

27.   Golden autumn leaves fall from tall conical crowns to reveal the straw-colored cones of the Tulip-tree; two seeds with single wings are detached. The Tulip-tree's duckbill buds are distinctive.

Viburnum

So complex as a class are the bold viburnums that no common name has evolved to designate this diverse group. Many viburnums are large spring-flowering shrubs which can be trained to develop a single-trunk tree form. We speak of the arrowwood, the black-haw, the withe-rod, the nanny-berry and dockmakie—all viburnums—scarcely aware that they are members of the same genus. *Viburnum* is the Latin name applied to the wayfaring-tree, a hairy leaved shrub of Europe. The group has many members ranging throughout the northern hemisphere. Several species bear remarkable resemblance to dogwoods. Common characteristics include habit, leaf arrangement, flowering season and berry color.

The pinnate leaves of viburnums are toothed. The buds are usually long, paralleling the stem and are frequently without scales. The seeds of viburnums are flattened like a coin while those of dogwood resemble tiny eggs or footballs.

Because it has black berries and stout spurs similar in form to those of the hawthorn, *Viburnum prunifolium* is familiarly known as black-haw (Illustration 28). Native to much of the eastern United States, it colonizes abandoned fields and pastures, providing food and protective thickets for game. This small tree, attractive throughout the year, is an additional native plant that may, with profit, be brought into our gardens. From rigid, horizontal, stiff-thorned branches, the black-haw's large, flat clusters of tiny white flowers, three to four inches across, are borne in early May. The flower buds are conspicuous all winter with their bulbous base and long tapering point. Before the leaves unfold, the flower buds open— pink at first, then fade to white. In late summer, the green berries turn pink and finally ripen blue-black.

Rarely exceeding twelve feet in height, the black-haw grows from a cluster of stems (ideal for bird nesting) unless trained to a single leader at an early age. The bark is checkered as with the persimmon. The foliage is small, up to three inches long, and of fine texture. In autumn the leaves become a subtle wine-red. Gray slender branches with long brown buds are revealed after the leaves fall. The branch pattern of winter increases the black-haw's attractiveness.

Boldness best characterizes the Siebold viburnum, *V. Sieboldii,* of Japan. Glossy dark green leaves, six inches long are borne on stout branches. Because of the tree's broad spread (to a height of twenty feet), and coarse-textured foliage, it can be planted at the far end of a narrow plot to dispel the feeling of distance. Another

137

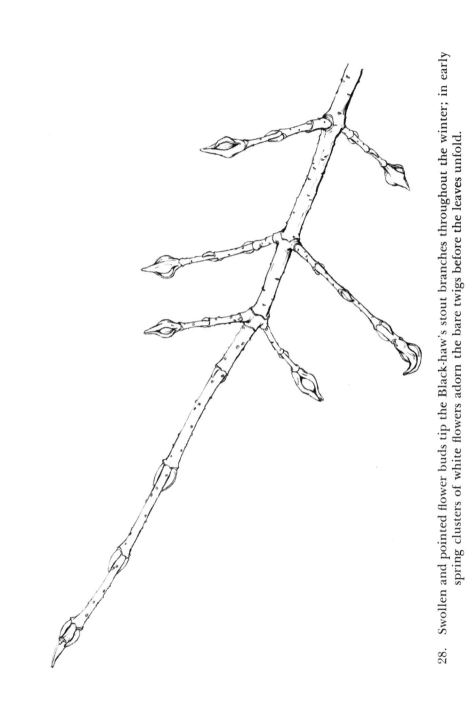

28. Swollen and pointed flower buds tip the Black-haw's stout branches throughout the winter; in early spring clusters of white flowers adorn the bare twigs before the leaves unfold.

reason sometimes offered for planting it away from the house is the strong odor of its blooms, (fragrant to some gardeners, overpowering to others). Clusters of white flowers, similar to those of black-haw, appear in late May amid the fresh bright foliage. This is an eye-appealing contrast of form and color.

Yellowwood
Cladrastis lutea

Graceful clusters of faintly fragrant white flowers, over a foot long, hang amid the fresh green foliage of the yellowwood in early June. Leaflets arranged alternately along the leafstalk form a compound leaf eight to twelve inches long. Concealed beneath the leafstalk during summer are brown, hairy, cone-shaped buds. These hidden buds are a distinctive feature of the yellowwood's branches which are smooth and uncluttered by leaf scars or short shoots.

The trunk sometimes divides into two or three large branches at a height of seven or eight feet. In silhouette the yellowwood is round-headed, with arching branches. The smooth gray bark resembles that of the beech. Nick the bark, however, and discover the yellowish wood. Zigzag, brittle branchlets provide the yellowwood with its

139

scientific name, derived from the Greek *klados,* branch, *thraustos,* fragile.

The yellowwood occurs principally in the luxuriant forests of the Cumberland Mountains of eastern Kentucky, but it can be grown successfully throughout the north. The blooms unfortunately fail to appear regularly each year, sometimes missing several seasons. This habit might be corrected while the tree is still young by allowing only a few flower clusters to bloom during the first few years. Pinch off excessive flowering shoots from the tips of the branchlets before the buds are fully expanded.

9

Possible Problems

In translating your ideal of landscape beauty into actuality you are certain to be confronted with problems. To maintain health, plants require water and mineral nutrients, in continuous supply but in moderate amounts. Withholding these plant-building materials checks growth. Providing them in superabundance overwhelms the plant. When you acquire a feeling for plants and their requirements you will experience one of the joys of gardening.

A tree's troubles can be revealed by a foliage abnormality such as yellowish color, dead spots, distortion, wilting, or dropping of leaves. Shoots or bark may be ruptured, discolored or shriveled. Usually a combination of characters or symptoms is needed before one can be sure of the nature of the difficulty.

Three common causes of injury to trees (or any plants)

are improper watering and nutrition and over-doses of insecticide or fungicide sprays. These errors may be due to mismanagement, inexperience, or simply failure to follow product package directions.

Gardeners frequently go to extremes with water—too much or too little.

WATERING

Newly planted trees, of course, need more careful watering than established trees with wide-ranging roots. All plants need air as well as water in the soil. Soil is composed of variously sized particles which, under favorable conditions, are coated with a film of moisture. Between the particles are spaces for air. If water occupies all of these tiny spaces (called pores) air is excluded and the tree literally drowns. A good rule of thumb is to water only when the plant needs it; that is, when the leaves show early signs of wilting or when the soil has become dry to the touch an inch below the surface.

When rainfall is scant and infrequent and temperatures are high, a listlessness comes over the garden. If soil moisture is not conserved or replenished, plants will dry up, eventually die. Trees that do come through a severe dry spell are almost certain to show effects the following growing season in retarded growth or failure to bloom. To assist plants in withstanding drought the gardener conserves soil moisture by providing adequate mulches of wood chips or other vegetable matter. If an ample supply of water is available, that is, if there are no municipal watering restrictions, remove the nozzle from your garden hose and let a slow stream of water soak into the soil under the drought-stricken trees overnight.

FOOD FOR GROWTH

Plant nutrition is to most of us a subject wrapped in mystery. When you apply a fertilizer high in nitrogen, the plant's leaves soon become deeper green. The chain reaction is beyond our present interest. Healthy plants are the objective in gardening. Results are what count. Fertilizers applied in too-heavy doses, or too frequently, or too late in the growing season, may produce poor results. Excessive feeding is worse than none at all.

Applications of fertilizers to soils are made to replace chemical elements used by the plants, and thereby to sustain or spur their growth. The elements which usually need to be replaced most often—even annually—are nitrogen, phosphorus, and potash, the N-P-K formula printed on bags of fertilizer. The remaining dozen or so lesser elements known to be necessary for healthy plant growth—called minor or trace elements—are usually adequately available in the soil or are supplied along with the major elements in most of the balanced, complete fertilizer products now on the market.

Over-dosing, on the assumption that a greater quantity of fertilizer will produce more or faster growth, often produces quite the opposite effect. Roots are "burned" when large amounts of fertilizer chemical come into contact with delicate root hairs. The remedy is to flush the soil with water to dissolve and carry away the toxic ingredients.

The increasing potency of modern chemical sprays and dusts for control of pests and diseases calls for increased caution in application and handling. Read carefully the package instructions and follow them closely. But use common sense, too. I should not attempt to spray, for instance, when the day is gusty. Usually breezes are not troublesome before ten o'clock in the morning.

Control of injurious insects is gained by thorough coverage of every part of the tree with recommended poisons at a time when the insects are vulnerable. Failure to time the application accurately will not only result in failure to halt the pests but may even heighten the potential danger. On the other hand, increasing the concentration of spray or dust runs the risk of injury to

144

plants. You may wish to call in a garden service man who makes tree care his specialty. If he is well-informed, experienced, and workmanlike, his charges will justify the services performed.

A FEW SPECIFICS

RECENTLY TRANSPLANTED TREES

When a tree is shifted to a new location the root system is disturbed; many of the root tips are severed. This means that the plant must grow new ones. You would do well in such cases to compensate for the root loss by pruning the top just after the transplanting operation. Thin out weak lateral branches and head back long side ones. Do not cut the leader, unless you want a round-topped, lower-growing specimen.

SUBURBAN GARDENS

Mass produced houses nowadays call for big construction operations. Garden sites are prepared with heavy machinery, according to fast-paced building production schedules. The soil structure has probably become violently disturbed through compaction and pulverizing, so that much time and effort must be spent to refit it for good gardening. A primary material in rebuilding soils

145

is organic matter, such as leaves, twigs, husks, manure, straw, and peat moss, to name just a few.

Disturbance of the water table (the level of the reservoir of soil water) is a common occurrence in land subdivisions that formerly were wooded. Trees "saved" by the home builder decline in vigor year after year even though no visible sign of injury to bark or branches is apparent. A layer of fill or a section of cut may be sufficient to create an untenable condition for normal tree life. The tree becomes weakened and succumbs more readily to attack by insect and disease.

Certain kinds of trees, such as elms and willows, are capable of withstanding additional deposits of soil about their roots. Most flowering tree species cannot tolerate this burden. If the disturbance consists of removal of part of the soil formerly occupied by roots, drought injury is likely to occur. You had best seek the advice of an experienced arborist before making deep cuts or fills.

GIRDLING ROOTS

"As the twig is bent so is the tree inclined" applies to roots as well. Roots near the trunk increase in diameter as the tree grows. Those that are twisted or bent during planting will continue growth in such contorted positions. In time the plant declines in vigor for no apparent

146

reason. If you dig about the trunk you are likely to find the source of the trouble—girdling roots—brought about by an acute constriction between large main roots and trunk. Remove the portion of root which exerts the pressure. Take care in future planting to spread out the roots so as to avoid similar conditions. Young container-grown trees, if left in such confinement too long, may develop girdling roots that will continue the habit in your garden unless you carefully "unwind" the roots before you plant.

REFLECTED LIGHT AND HEAT

Contemporary architecture employs large surfaces of materials that reflect the sun's heat and light rays. The foliage of trees planted in sites that receive this extra radiation sometimes turns brown and, in extreme cases, the plant dies. This is the province of the recent science of microclimatology, a study affecting every gardener. You can protect plants, in general, with peat moss, and from excess sun with screens placed around them. Light-colored pavements and walls also mirror heat and light rays onto sensitive foliage. Summer and winter are critical periods, but danger exists during any season.

147

LIGHTNING

Tall trees which are virtually irreplacable ought to be protected by properly grounded lightning rods. This is definitely a job for a professional arborist.

GIRDLED BARK

Bark is the protective skin for woody plants. Just under the bark are the masses of tiny tubes that conduct water-soluble nutrients from the roots up to the branches, twigs, leaves and buds. When large patches of bark are injured or torn off the trunk, the tree's "plumbing system" is disrupted and immediate efforts must be made to reestablish contact between roots and top. Inarching and bridge-grafting are two methods of doing this, but the wise amateur will leave these operations to the tree expert.

To avoid recurrence, install guards between the trunk and the path of danger, such as along highways or where heavy machinery is likely to make contact. Rodents, another source of bark depredation, may be poisoned, repelled by chemicals, fenced out, or foiled by removing the soil mulch which harbors them in winter.

V. Like Japanese lanterns, Golden-chain's flower clusters hang amid the fresh green foliage in late May.

INSECTS

Sucking, chewing, mining, and boring insects are controlled by natural predators, or, in epidemic invasions, by chemicals. Since World War II many organic insecticide compounds have found favor among nurserymen and orchardists for the efficient control of pernicious insects. For the home gardener some of these chemicals, such as malathion, methoxychlor, lindane, and dieldrin, are excellent; others may be risky to handle and may not be efficient unless used with professional exactness. Many of the old-fashioned sprays and dusts such as nicotine sulfate and pyrethrum are still recommended. Timing and thoroughness are of major importance. Watch your local newspaper for timely bulletins from your county agricultural agent.

DISEASES

Flowering trees, like other plants, are heir to a number of harmful and sometimes fatal diseases. Many of them are harder to control than most insects. The adage about an ounce of prevention applies perfectly to disease problems, and for that the cardinal rule is SANITATION— promptly raking up or pruning off and destroying all infected leaves, twigs and such. Among the leading fungi-

149

FLOWERING TREES

cides for garden use are captan, zineb, maneb, ferbam, phaltan, as well as antibiotics. The county agent is your best source for exact recommendations as to materials and tree-spray schedules for your area. (Also see discussion under Rosaceous Diseases later in this chapter.)

WEEDS AND VINES

The competition among plants for light and moisture is intense. Unwanted plants are insidious and aggressive. Healthy weeds at least indicate that the soil will support vegetation. You can control weeds with a combination of vigilance and modern herbicides. Poison ivy, which invariably seems to grow right up the trunk of a favorite tree, must be rooted out or attacked with brush-killing chemicals. Do not burn poison ivy vines or leaves. The smoke is dangerous.

LANGUISHING TREES

A tree that fails to respond to any treatment may have been set too deep at planting time. Replant it at the next favorable season, taking care to set the root ball the depth that it grew in the nursery. Avoid putting a lot of fresh organic materials, such as manure or leaf mold, in the bottom of the hole. These materials decay and shrink, causing the tree to settle below the optimum level. The planting hole should be only the depth of the root ball (although the soil should be loosened several inches deeper).

ROSE FAMILY NOTES

Cherries and crabapples are well-known members of the rose family, that vast tribe of plants so important to man for food and ornament, so widespread in distribution throughout the world, and so large in number of species. Shadbush, pear, peach, mountain-ash, hawthorn and photinia are other relatives of the garden rose. All are spring-blooming small trees with large, usually flat clusters of five-petaled flowers borne with or before the appearance of the leaves. Since the rose family members have similar and sometimes particular cultural requirements, they are discussed here as a separate part of this general "cultural problems" chapter.

Trees of the rose family reach their best development in sunny locations where the soil is well drained. A garden soil that sustains a healthy crop of weeds is an excellent site for planting rosaceous flowering trees. Fertility can be adjusted as needed, but the soil should be sufficiently loose so that water does not stand on it for hours after a rain or watering. There should be

151

enough humus in the soil to sustain an ample moisture content during brief dry spells.

Most flowering trees make satisfactory recovery from transplanting when their roots are balled and burlaped (B & B). This B & B rule applies to specimens of blooming size, not to saplings—which are planted bare-root while dormant. Certainly B & B should be used when moving trees during the growing season. Nearly all rosaceous trees, except possibly certain cherries, belong in this category. Specific instructions for planting B & B stock are given in Chapter 11.

Field mice and rabbits find the bark of crabapples especially to their liking. Mice spend the winter in a thick mulch beneath the branches. Rabbits gnaw bark as high as they can reach, which may be pretty high when snowfall is abundant. Mouse injury may be avoided by poisoning the mice with special bait or by removing the mulch from the immediate vicinity of the trunk in late autumn. Rabbits may be repelled by painting a solution of rosin and denatured ethyl alcohol on the base of the trunk, and to a height of twenty-four inches.

Certain insects and diseases are peculiar to rosaceous plants. Everyone is familiar with tent caterpillar nests on black cherry trees and the orange galls on red-cedars in late spring or early summer. The first is caused by an insect that chews the tender new leaves; the latter is a fungous disease that spends part of its life on hawthorn or crabapple leaves.

In late summer the pestiferous tent caterpillars lay their eggs near the crotches of young branches of cherries and crabapples. Throughout the winter these black shiny egg masses resemble wads of gum wrapped around the bare twigs. If the eggs are not detected and rubbed off, or treated with a dormant oil spray, the caterpillars will emerge in April and begin to form their tents. By early May the tents will be quite large and considerable leaf damage will have been done, so get after them as early as possible with strong jet sprays of lead arsenate or malathion.

Scale insects suck the sap and weaken the tree. These are best controlled by an oil spray applied just prior to the swelling of buds in late winter or early spring. The spray is a high-grade petroleum oil emulsion. The object is to apply it uniformly and have it form a film over the bark. Choose a calm sunny day when the temperature is above 40 degrees. Aim the sprayer (with nozzle set for a fine mist) at the center of the tree, working up the several branches. The emulsion streams down the branches so you must work rapidly. If you are getting good coverage the bark will glisten.

153

FLOWERING TREES

Rosaceous Diseases

In sections where red-cedars grow, a fungous disease, called cedar-apple rust, is likely to become established. Slimy orange galls are seen on the cedars in May or June. This is the most conspicuous stage of the rust. In mid-summer, blemishes occur on crabapple or hawthorn leaves. If you have this problem, you can either get rid of the red-cedars or forget about growing hawthorns and crabapples, especially the American species.

During the growing season, you may notice a rosaceous plant on which some of the leaves are colored orange or brown and the ends of the shoots shriveled and discolored. This is caused by a bacterial disease, called fireblight. The bacteria are spread by insects, rain and wind. Sanitation once again is the recommended procedure for control. Once a month during the growing season, inspect the branches of all rosaceous plants. With care, prune all infected branches and burn them. Sterilize the blade after each cut by dipping it in a disinfectant. Fireblight often attacks trees with soft succulent wood brought about by an overabundance of moisture or an immoderate use of nitrogenous fertilizer.

154

10

Grow Your Own Flowering Trees

Seeds are Nature's way of perpetuating a species—insurance against extermination. Of more practical importance to gardeners, however, is the fact that trees grown from seed develop deep well-branched root systems which provide life insurance for the tree in dry periods. The seedling plant also carries inheritance factors from another individual plant, as well as from the one on which the seed was borne. Therefore it probably will not develop as an imitation of the seed-bearing parent but is likely to vary in some or many characteristics. This, of course, is not an advantage if you wish to have exact copies of particular plants; to achieve that, you must employ methods of vegetative (asexual) propagation such as cuttings, grafting and layering (which are discussed at the end of this chapter). The contrast is striking between a hybrid plant and one in which pollination was left to chance. Growing shrubs or trees from seed can become a most fascinating and fruitful adventure.

Preparations

As soon as a tree's fruits have become ripe the time is at hand for collecting the seeds. Certain fruits are attractive to wild life—birds and rodents—and must be protected. A sure sign of ripeness in any species is the beginning of fruit drop in autumn. In brief, when fruits are brightly colored, soft, or brittle, they are ready for gathering.

Have a convenient receptable—basket or polyethylene sack—for transporting the tree-fruit treasure to the kitchen sink or table. Husks should be removed and the seeds cleaned. If the covering is fleshy, the pulp can be allowed to soak overnight so that it can be more readily separated. Agitating the fruit in water by means of an electric mixer or blender sometimes answers the purpose if the seed coat is tough and the pulp is soft. The good seeds sink while the worthless ones float when free of pulp. The fluid is poured off and the good seed recovered, air dried and then sowed, or stored in a cool dry place until time permits sowing.

The seed bed usually is made in a bulb pan—a large-sized shallow clay pot commonly used for forcing spring bulbs. Put a piece of crock over the drainage hole, or use a layer of coarse gravel. Add a loose and not too fertile potting soil (a popular mixture consists of equal parts of soil, sand and peat). Other materials such as vermiculite and perlite can be used instead of sand. The seeds now are broadcast or drilled over the leveled surface and are covered with a shallow layer of sand or milled sphagnum moss. Mark the rows with clear labels. A covering of moist burlap, a pane of glass or a sheet of polyethylene may be used to keep the surface from drying out. If there is danger of mice, the whole container should be protected by quarter-inch mesh hardware cloth and placed where it can be inspected frequently. A darkened place not too close to heat should be selected. If the seed bed becomes too warm, the soil will dry out and will require frequent syringing.

How to Handle Seeds

Seeds of different species vary in the time needed for germination and in the treatment they require. According to their responses, seed may be classified into the following categories of handling: 1. Clean and sow as soon as ripe or store in a cool dry place and sow when convenient. 2. Soften the seed coat by mechanical or chemical means. 3. Place the seeds in a moist medium and then (A) subject them to cold temperatures for a specified period, or (B) leave them at room temperature for a certain period before subjecting them to cold. 4. Combine treatments 2 and 3A, by softening the seed coat and exposing the seeds to cold temperatures.

Seeds that may be sowed at any convenient time and which will germinate within a few days or weeks do not have dormancy, that is to say, any factors which impede their germination. Such trees as white-alder, catalpa, photinia, sourwood and willow belong in this category. The seeds of these trees are considered easy to germinate.

Seeds with hard coats impervious to water constitute the second group which comprises chiefly legumes, such as black locust, redbud, silk-tree and yellowwood. The simplest method is to pour boiling water into a jar containing the seed and allow to stand overnight. Other techniques involve chipping the seed coat with a knife or softening it in concentrated sulphuric acid. These methods have certain obvious hazards and are not recommended for amateur use.

In the third category are seeds whose coats are normal but whose growing points are not activated until the seed has been subjected to cold temperatures, usually about forty degrees, for a month or more (a good place is in the vegetable bin of the refrigerator). These seeds are also somewhat selective of the moist medium in which they undergo this treatment, some giving better responses in sand, some in peat, while others prefer a mixture of sand and peat.

a. Seeds that require moist sand.

Seed	Temperature	Days	Special Treatment
Lilac	41° F.	30-90	
Tree of heaven	41	60	
Olive, Russian-	41	90	
Goldenrain-tree	41	90	Acid 60
Chestnut, horse-	41	120	
Cherry, black-	41	120	soak dry seeds acid 30

b. Seeds that require moist peat.

Peach	35-45	45-90	
Tulip-tree	32-50	70	soil overwinter
Ash, mountain-, European	33	90	peat pH4. Warm & cold
Service-berry	33-41	90-120	
Magnolia evergreen	41, or 50	90-120, or 120-150 days	

159

c. Seeds that respond to any mixture of moist sand and peat.

Pear	32-50	60-90
Birch	32-50	60-90
Crabapple	32-50	30-90

Seeds of the following group require a warm period (room temperatures) prior to a cold period in which to sprout first the root and then the shoot.

	Warm Period		Cold Period	
Dogwood, flowering	77°	30-60 days	33°	120-150 days
Hawthorn	70-80	several weeks	41	75-90
Dogwood, giant	68-86	60	41	60
Silverbell	56-86	60-120	33-41	60-90
Linden, European littleleaf	59-77	120-150	34-41	120-150 (sand or peat)
Haw, black-	68-86	120-200	41	30-45 (peat, or sand and peat)
Fringe-tree			41	overwinter (sand and peat)

CARE OF SEEDLINGS

As soon as the tiny seedlings appear, the container should be brought into the light in order to keep the fledglings sturdy. Weeds must be promptly removed.

Once a goodly number of tree seedlings have reached the true leaf stage, they may, in turn, be pricked off (transplanted) to a seedling flat where better conditions for rapid growth are provided.

The young plants must be kept growing vigorously. Assuming that germination begins in spring, you should keep the seedlings indoors—preferably in a greenhouse or under sash or lath—so that sudden or excessive changes of temperature are not permitted to check their development. Then, when weather warms up, they may be placed outside under lath shade. They may be kept there for a year or two. Frequent syringing during hot sunny days helps to keep the temperature moderate. When the days begin to shorten and night temperatures fall, the young plants ought to receive cover at night but all the sunshine available during the day. Watering should be less frequent in fall so that the tender growth hardens off properly.

VEGETATIVE PROPAGATION

To obtain new plants that possess the characters of the original plant, it is necessary to take shoots or buds and to stimulate the formation of roots on them or to unite them with compatible rootstocks.

Many plants may be increased by cuttings taken as

161

greenwood in midsummer or as hardwood during the cold season. Both methods work best when you have special facilities, such as a greenhouse bench, for rooting the cuttings (in a light, porous soil mixture). The advantage of summer propagation is that the sun provides the heat. A high humidity level is essential to keep the cuttings from wilting until they form their own roots. Some kinds of woody plants, such as oaks, crabapples and red-blooming rhododendrons, do not readily strike root from cuttings, but require grafting on compatible stock. An advantage of hardwood cuttings is that the cutting bench can be kept in use after the softwood cuttings are rooted and removed; however heat must then be supplied throughout the winter. Hardwood cuttings—tip growth roughly eight inches long—of deciduous trees are taken after leaves have fallen and are stored in boxes of moist sand until calluses have formed. They are then ready to be stuck in the cutting bench. This is done in late winter.

Grafting is a technique that unites the shoot of a desired plant with a compatible root system. There are few skilled practitioners of this art these days. Grafting is done (1) to modify the habit (appearance) of the plant, as for example in dwarfing a plant, (2) to improve the adaptability of a plant to temperature conditions, drainage or type of soil, and (3) to increase the regeneration of a plant by assisting it with the roots of another plant. The delicate operation involves uniting the living sap layers, a technique that does not always prove successful.

BUDDING AND LAYERING

A modification of grafting is budding, the art of inserting an undeveloped shoot under the bark of a pencil-sized stem. The same probabilities apply as with grafting. Budding has the advantage that it may be done in the open garden.

Layering is simply a form of propagation by cuttings. The difference is that roots are encouraged to form on a branch while it is still attached to the tree. Early spring is the best time to start. The first step is wounding the branch: use a sharp knife to remove a narrow strip of bark, two or three inches long, from the lower side of the branch. (Be careful to remove only a sliver of outer bark). Make this wound at least twelve to eighteen inches from the tip of a straight, young side branch. Then, if the branch is low growing it can be bent down to the ground and partly buried (including, of course, the wounded area), so that a foot or more of the branch tip protrudes. This is called simple layering. Pile more soil or stones over

163

the buried part to help hold it down (or anchor it with a U-shaped piece of wire). Keep the soil moist. If the branch is high or for some other reason cannot be bent down to the ground, you can air-layer it; that is, pack the wounded area of the branch with moistened sphagnum moss. Encase this in a sealed wrapping or "envelope" of polyethylene film to retain the moisture in the moss. Rooting time will vary from a few weeks to several months. When a good root mass has formed—usually by late summer or early fall—the branch is severed just below the new roots and the new tree is planted where wanted.

11

Transplanting

The moving of trees to their permanent location in the garden involves several variables: site, species, season and skill.

SITE

The home gardener is limited by the soils of his property. Fortunately most flowering trees are not finicky about the soils in which they grow. A few species may need or prefer some particular conditions such as exceptionally well-drained soil or a rather wet soil, fertile or almost sterile soil, alkaline or acid soil. If your property cannot meet the demands of these particular trees, the simplest solution is to grow other species.

Nearly all trees grow best in well-drained soils. Certain species, however, tolerate wet soils, including the gray

165

birch, white fringe-tree, white-alder and sweet-bay magnolia. Fertile soil is important, of course, but some species of flowering trees grow quite well in poor soils; these include gray birch, catalpa, black cherry, black locust, beach plum, Russian-olive, silk-tree, and the controversial tree-of-heaven. Limestone soil favors many species, but acid soils seem to be needed for the best development of the white-alder, Franklin-tree, sweetbay magnolia and sourwood.

Species

Even though flowering trees may not be too particular about their environment, they nevertheless respond differently to different handling. Long experience shows that a score of plants are best moved only with their roots balled and burlaped (B & B) and further, that about one-half of these should be transferred only while the plants are still small. The great majority of flowering trees may be transplanted in the dormant period even in large sizes without a soil ball around their roots (bare-root or BR). Recovery following planting is rapid for many species, only moderately good for others. The following is a list of some of the flowering trees that should be transplanted with care, B & B:

Birch, gray *Betula populifolia*

Cherry, Japanese	*Prunus serrulata*
Cherry, rosebud	*Prunus subhirtella* var. *pendula*
Crape-myrtle	*Lagerstroemia indica*
Crabapples	*Malus* species
Dogwoods, flowering	*Cornus* species
Franklin-tree	*Franklinia alatamaha*
Hawthorns	*Crataegus* species
Maackia	*Maackia* species
Magnolias	*Magnolia* species
Redbud	*Cercis canadensis*
Scholar-tree	*Sophora japonica*
Snowbells	*Styrax* species
Sourwood	*Oxydendrum arboreum*
Tulip-tree	*Liriodendron Tulipifera*

SEASON. The dormant period, when deciduous trees are leafless, undoubtedly is the safest time for transplanting. This period extends for about seven months, usually from mid-October to mid-May, in the Middle Atlantic states. As long as the soil is not frozen and while it is in good tilth, it is in proper condition for root activity. If the weather remains sufficiently warm during the winter, new roots develop even while the tops are without leaves. This is why some gardeners prefer fall transplanting—

167

because of the head start provided for the root system. The soil, moreover, is warmer in late fall than in early spring. Nevertheless, most people plant in the spring, probably because that is the season when the impulse for gardening is strongest. In any case, do not plant unless the soil is workable. To test for workability, take a handful of soil and squeeze it gently but firmly into a ball. Let it drop from waist height. If it holds together on impact, the soil is too wet to work; if the ball shatters into small clods, it is in good condition for transplanting.

Transplanting B & B, in which the root system is held in its original soil ball and wrapped in burlap, is recommended for flowering trees which experience has shown are difficult to transplant. It is also used when moving woody plants out-of-season; that is during the growing period while the leaves are fully developed. Moreover, it may be employed for all flowering trees, if specified, but the planting cost will be correspondingly greater owing to special handling.

The season of transplanting is limited by (1) the weather and soil conditions, (2) the species, type and size of plant and (3) the method of transplanting; in brief by the environment, the plant and the skill of the gardener. Even though, under ideal conditions, any plant may be transplanted any day of the year, you seldom are

168

so fortunate as to have ideal conditions. The general rule, then, is to plan carefully the job that is to be done, having tools, materials and helpers available and in readiness at the time you schedule the operation. Finally the weather itself has an immediate effect upon the result. Hot sunshine wilts tender leaves if foliage is expanding or fully developed. Choose an overcast day, or do the transplanting late in the afternoon.

SKILL. Dig a hole twice as wide as the width of the B & B root ball, but no deeper. The plant should stand at about the same depth it grew in the nursery. When the tree is properly set in the hole with its best aspect to the front and the trunk vertical, a shovelful or two of backfill soil is tamped against the root ball to steady it in place. A handful or two of powdered dolomitic limestone mixed with the backfill gives the roots of most plants a good start. A couple of shovelfulls of well-decayed humus or other organic matter mixed thoroughly in the backfill is also beneficial. The burlap may be turned back at the top of the rootball but it is not necessary to remove all of the burlap since roots will grow through it. Take care not to crack the soil ball lest the roots be injured. If there is doubt about the compactness of the root ball, the best solution is to leave the burlap intact.

169

In backfilling, the soil may be stomped into place or it may be puddled. The main thing is to eliminate air pockets and then assure sufficient water in the root zone. A shallow bowl should be left about the plant to catch rain water and irrigation during the tree's first critical weeks after transplanting.

A tall tree should be staked so that the wind will not rock it and break the roots. Initial pruning involves the removal of broken branchlets and the training of basic scaffold branches. Not for several years should further pruning be necessary.

Water, however, is a different story. The need for water changes with the weather and the development of the roots. Freshly transplanted trees have limited root systems and so need watering even in short drought periods. But do not drown them. Once established, the tree will forage for itself except during protracted spells of heat and drought. Mulching with wood chips or other vegetable matter is a good way to conserve soil moisture as well as keep roots cool.

12

Maintenance Pruning

Pruning is the intelligent practice of removing any portion of a plant for the purpose of improving it in some way. It is an art or skill that may be acquired through experience. When the aspiring pruner discovers that each kind of plant behaves differently, he is understandably perplexed. A novice should seek the advice of his county agricultural agent, an arborist, or an experienced landscape maintenance man. Failing the assistance of such skilled horticulturists, he should leave the plant alone. Flowers and fruits will develop if the tree is healthy.

A few words of encouragement, however, may be helpful. Certain pruning practices are easy to understand. Prime among these is removal of dead, weak or injured branches. Removal of large branches should be left to the expert who has the proper tools and skill (and insurance) for the handling of such operations.

The best time to prune a tree is when it is young. Undesirable growth is then easy to cut off or even nip off with the fingernail, and the pruning scars are infinitesimal. In pruning to spur the production of flowers, inspect the tree when it is in bloom. Look for the position of the flower on the twig. This will indicate the type of wood that should be stimulated. Flower buds develop either along the shoots or at or near the tips. The shoots may be long or short, depending upon their position and the age of the wood on which they are borne. If the flowers arise on twigs of the current season, as with the silk-tree and Franklin-tree, new growth may be stimulated each year during the dormant season by removing a large proportion of the past season's shoots. The pruner should use judgment in the amount of wood he removes, since removal of all of the young shoots is likely to delay blooming for a year or so.

With trees which bear flowers on shoots developed during the previous growing season—including of course the early-blooming trees—pruning may be confined to restraining the growth of long shoots during the growing season. This type of pruning is called heading-in. When both flowers and leaves arise from the same bud, vigorous

172

shoots here and there may be headed-in before the wood has begun to harden in early summer and the flower buds have begun to form for the following year. Again, a too-thorough job of heading-in may reduce or postpone bloom for a year or more. Remember that most flowering trees, once they attain the blooming stage, require little pruning.

Appendix I: Tree Traits

HEIGHT

Alder, white-	*Clethra barbinervis*
Birch, gray	*Betula populifolia*
Buckthorn, woolly	*Bumelia lanuginosa*
Cherry, cornelian-	*Cornus mas*
Cherry, Fuji	*Prunus incisa*
Cherry, Oriental	*Prunus serrulata*
Crabapple, Arnold	*Malus arnoldiana*
Crabapple, carmine	*Malus atrosanguinea*
Crabapple, Dorothea	*Malus* 'Dorothea'
Crabapple, flowering-, Japanese	*Malus floribunda*
Crabapple, Katherine	*Malus* 'Katherine'
Crabapple, Lemoine	*Malus purpurea* 'Lemoinei'
Crabapple, Parkman	*Malus Halliana* 'Parkmanii'
Crabapple, Sargent	*Malus Sargentii*
Crabapple, Scheidecker	*Malus Scheideckeri*
Crabapple, tea	*Malus hupehensis*
Dogwood, Chinese	*Cornus Kousa*
Dogwood, flowering	*Cornus florida*

174

Dogwood, giant	*Cornus controversa*
Ehretia, heliotrope	*Ehretia thyrsiflora*
Franklin-tree	*Franklinia alatamaha*
Fringe-tree, Chinese	*Chionanthus retusus*
Fringe-tree, white	*Chionanthus virginicus*
Golden-chain, Waterer's	*Laburnum Watereri*
Haw, black-	*Viburnum prunifolium*
Hawthorn, Washington	*Crataegus Phaenopyrum*
Lilac, Peking	*Syringa pekinensis*
Maackia	*Maackia chinensis*
Magnolia, saucer	*Magnolia Soulangiana*
Magnolia, sweetbay	*Magnolia virginiana*
Olive, Russian-	*Elaeagnus angustifolia*
Peach	*Prunus Persica*
Photinia	*Photinia villosa*
Plum, beach	*Prunus maritima*
Plum, purple-leaved	*Prunus cerasifera* 'Pissardii'
Redbud	*Cercis canadensis*
Service-berry, smooth	*Amelanchier laevis*
Silk-tree, hardy	*Albizia Julibrissin* var. *rosea*
Silverbell, Carolina	*Halesia carolina*
Snowbell, Japanese	*Styrax japonica*
Smoke-tree	*Cotinus Coggygria*

BETWEEN 20 AND 40 FEET IN HEIGHT

Ash, mountain-, Korean	*Sorbus alnifolia*
Beebee-tree, Korean	*Evodia Daniellii*
Catalpa, Chinese	*Catalpa ovata*
Cherry, rosebud	*Prunus subhirtella* var. *pendula*
Cherry, Yoshino	*Prunus yedoensis*
Chestnut, Chinese	*Castanea mollissima*

175

FLOWERING TREES

Crabapple, Bechtel	*Malus ioensis* 'Plena'
Crabapple, cutleaf	*Malus toringoides*
Crabapple, flowering-, Chinese	*Malus spectabilis* 'Riversii'
Crabapple, slender Siberian	*Malus baccata* 'Gracilis'
Epaulette-tree	*Pterostyrax hispida*
Goldenrain-tree	*Koelreuteria paniculata*
Idesia	*Idesia polycarpa*
Magnolia, anise	*Magnolia salicifolia*
Magnolia, evergreen	*Magnolia grandiflora*
Magnolia, Kobus	*Magnolia Kobus*
Magnolia, Yulan	*Magnolia denudata*
Pear, Callery	*Pyrus Calleryana*
Raisin-tree, Japanese	*Hovenia dulcis*
Silverbell, mountain	*Halesia monticola*
Snowbell, fragrant	*Styrax Obassia*
Sourwood	*Oxydendrum arboreum*
Stewartia, Japanese	*Stewartia Pseudo-Camellia*
Stewartia, Korean	*Stewartia koreana*
Viburnum, Siebold	*Viburnum Sieboldii*
Yellowwood	*Cladrastis lutea*

GREATER THAN 40 FEET TALL

Buckeye, sweet	*Aesculus octandra*
Cherry, black	*Prunus serotina*
Cherry, Sargent	*Prunus Sargentii*
Chestnut, horse-, double	*Aesculus Hippocastanum* 'Baumannii'
Chestnut, horse-, ruby	*Aesculus carnea* 'Briotii'
Linden, Crimean	*Tilia euchlora*
Linden, European largeleaf	*Tilia platyphyllos*
Linden, European littleleaf	*Tilia cordata*

176

Linden, pendent silver	*Tilia petiolaris*
Linden, silver	*Tilia tomentosa*
Locust, black	*Robinia Pseudoacacia*
Scholar-tree, Chinese	*Sophora japonica*
Tree of heaven	*Ailanthus altissima*
Tulip-tree	*Liriodendron Tulipifera*

SILHOUETTE

CONICAL (NARROW PYRAMIDAL)

Ash, mountain-, European	*Sorbus Aucuparia*
Ash, mountain-, Korean	*Sorbus alnifolia*
Birch, gray	*Betula populifolia*
Crabapple, cutleaf	*Malus toringoides*
Dove-tree	*Davidia involucrata*
Ehretia, heliotrope	*Ehretia thyrsiflora*
Franklin-tree	*Franklinia alatamaha*
Lilac, tree-, Japanese	*Syringa amurensis* var. *japonica*
Linden, silver	*Tilia tomentosa*
Magnolia, anise	*Magnolia salicifolia*
Magnolia, evergreen	*Magnolia grandiflora*
Magnolia, Kobus	*Magnolia Kobus*
Raisin-tree, Japanese	*Hovenia dulcis*
Snowbell, fragrant	*Styrax Obassia*
Tulip-tree	*Liriodendron Tulipifera*

OVAL-SHAPED TREES (NARROW WITH ROUNDED SUMMIT)

Catalpa, Chinese	*Catalpa ovata*
Epaulette-tree	*Pterostyrax hispida*
Linden, European littleleaf	*Tilia cordata*

177

FLOWERING TREES

Pear, Callery	*Pyrus Calleryana*
Service-berry, smooth	*Amelanchier laevis*
Sourwood	*Oxydendrum arboreum*
Stewartia, Japanese	*Stewartia Pseudo-Camellia*
Stewartia, Korean	*Stewartia koreana*

ROUND-HEADED

Buckeye, sweet	*Aesculus octandra*
Cherry, black	*Prunus serotina*
Cherry, Fuji	*Prunus incisa*
Cherry, Yoshino	*Prunus yedoensis*
Chestnut, Chinese	*Castanea mollissima*
Chestnut, horse-, double	*Aesculus Hippocastanum* 'Baumannii'
Chestnut, horse-, ruby	*Aesculus carnea* 'Briotii'
Crabapple, Arnold	*Malus arnoldiana*
Crabapple, Bechtel	*Malus ioensis* 'Plena'
Crabapple, flowering-, Chinese	*Malus spectabilis* 'Riversii'
Crabapple, Parkman	*Malus Halliana* 'Parkmanii'
Crabapple, slender Siberian	*Malus baccata* 'Gracilis'
Empress-tree	*Paulownia tomentosa*
Fringe-tree, Chinese	*Chionanthus retusus*
Fringe-tree, white	*Chionanthus virginicus*
Goldenrain-tree	*Koelreuteria paniculata*
Haw, black-	*Viburnum prunifolium*
Hawthorn, Washington	*Crataegus Phaenopyrum*
Idesia	*Idesia polycarpa*
Lilac, Peking	*Syringa pekinensis*
Linden, Crimean	*Tilia euchlora*
Linden, European largeleaf	*Tilia platyphyllos*
Locust, black	*Robinia Pseudoacacia*

178

Magnolia, saucer	*Magnolia Soulangiana*
Magnolia, Yulan	*Magnolia denudata*
Olive, Russian-	*Elaeagnus angustifolia*
Plum, beach	*Prunus maritima*
Plum, purple-leaved	*Prunus cerasifera* 'Pissardii'
Redbud	*Cercis candensis*
Silverbells	*Halesia* species
Smoke-tree	*Cotinus Coggygria*
Snowbell, Japanese	*Styrax japonica*
Tree of heaven	*Ailanthus altissima*
Viburnum, Siebold	*Viburnum Sieboldii*

BROAD-SPREADING TREES WITH HORIZONTAL BRANCHES

Alder, white-	*Clethra barbinervis*
Beebee-tree, Korean	*Evodia Daniellii*
Buckthorn, woolly	*Bumelia lanuginosa*
Cherry, cornelian-	*Cornus mas*
Cherry, Oriental-flowering	*Prunus serrulata*
Cherry, Sargent	*Prunus Sargentii*
Crabapple, carmine	*Malus atrosanguinea*
Crabapple, Dorothea	*Malus* 'Dorothea'
Crabapple, flowering-, Japanese	*Malus floribunda*
Crabapple, Katherine	*Malus* 'Katherine'
Crabapple, Lemoine	*Malus purpurea* 'Lemoinei'
Crabapple, Sargent	*Malus Sargentii*
Crabapple, Scheidecker	*Malus Scheideckeri*
Crabapple, tea	*Malus hupehensis*
Dogwood, Chinese	*Cornus Kousa*
Dogwood, flowering	*Cornus florida*
Dogwood, giant	*Cornus controversa*
Golden-chain, Waterer's	*Laburnum Watereri*

179

FLOWERING TREES

Maackia	*Maackia chinensis*
Magnolia, sweetbay	*Magnolia virginiana*
Peach	*Prunus Persica*
Photinia	*Photinia villosa*
Silk-tree, hardy	*Albizia Julibrissin* var. *rosea*
Yellowwood	*Cladrastis lutea*

ARCHING PENDENT BRANCHES (FOUNTAIN TYPE)

Cherry, rosebud	*Prunus subhirtella* var. *pendula*
Linden, pendent silver	*Tilia petiolaris*

COLOR OF FLOWER

RED

Chestnut, horse-, ruby	*Aesculus carnea* 'Briotii'
Crabapple, carmine	*Malus atrosanguinea*
Peach, red, semi-double	*Prunus Persica* 'Rubra-plena'
Peach, deep red, semi-double	*Prunus Persica* 'Camelliaeflora'
Peach, crimson, double	*Prunus Persica* 'Magnifica'

PINK

Cherry, Oriental	*Prunus serrulata* 'Kwanzan'
Cherry, rosebud	*Prunus subhirtella* var. *pendula*
Cherry, Sargent	*Prunus Sargentii*
Crabapple, Betchel	*Malus ioensis* 'Plena'
Crabapple, Dorothea	*Malus* 'Dorothea'
Crabapple, Parkman	*Malus Halliana* 'Parkmanii'
Crabapple, Scheidecker	*Malus Scheideckeri*
Magnolia, Rustica	*Magnolia Soulangiana* 'Rubra'
Peach, pink, semi-double	*Prunus Persica* 'Dianthiflora'

VI. Orange throated green goblets attract pollinating insects to the Tulip-tree in May as the square lobed leaves are unfolding.

Peach, pink, double	*Prunus Persica* 'Duplex'
Plum, purple-leaved	*Prunus cerasifera* 'Pissardii'
Redbud	*Cercis canadensis*
Silk-tree, hardy	*Albizia Julibrissin* var. *rosea*
Silverbell, mountain	*Halesia monticola* 'Rosea'

RED-PURPLE OR LAVENDER

Crabapple, Lemoine	*Malus purpurea* 'Lemoinei'
Empress-tree	*Paulownia tomentosa*

YELLOW

Birch, gray	*Betula populifolia*
Buckeye, sweet	*Aesculus octandra*
Cherry, cornelian-	*Cornus mas*
Chestnut, Chinese	*Castanea mollissima*
Golden-chain, Waterer's	*Laburnum Watereri*
Goldenrain-tree	*Koelreuteria paniculata*
Olive, Russian-	*Elaeagnus angustifolia*
Scholar-tree, Chinese	*Sophora japonica*

CREAMY WHITE TO GREEN

Buckthorn, woolly	*Bumelia lanuginosa*
Idesia	*Idesia polycarpa*
Lilac, Japanese	*Syringa amurensis* var. *japonica*
Lilac, Peking	*Syringa pekinensis*
Linden, Crimean	*Tilia euchlora*
Linden, European largeleaf	*Tilia platyphyllos*
Linden, European littleleaf	*Tilia cordata*
Linden, pendent silver	*Tilia petiolaris*
Linden, silver	*Tilia tomentosa*
Maackia	*Maackia chinensis*

FLOWERING TREES

Raisin-tree, Japanese	*Hovenia dulcis*
Smoke-tree	*Cotinus Coggygria*
Sourwood	*Oxydendrum arboreum*
Tree of heaven	*Ailanthus altissima*
Tulip-tree	*Liriodendron Tulipifera*

WHITE

Alder, white-	*Clethra barbinervis*
Ash, mountain-, European	*Sorbus Aucuparia*
Ash, mountain-, Korean	*Sorbus alnifolia*
Beebee-tree, Korean	*Evodia Daniellii*
Catalpa, Chinese	*Catalpa ovata*
Cherry, black	*Prunus serotina*
Cherry, Fuji	*Prunus incisa*
Cherry, Oriental	*Prunus serrulata* 'Sirotae' and 'Amanogawa'
Cherry, Yoshino	*Prunus yedoensis*
Chestnut, horse-, double-flowering	*Aesculus hippocastanum* 'Baumannii'
Crabapple, Arnold	*Malus arnoldiana*
Crabapple, cutleaf	*Malus toringoides*
Crabapple, flowering-, Chinese	*Malus spectabilis* 'Riversii'
Crabapple, flowering-, Japanese	*Malus floribunda*
Crabapple, Katherine	*Malus* 'Katherine'
Crabapple, Sargent	*Malus Sargentii*
Crabapple, slender Siberian	*Malus baccata* 'Gracilis'
Crabapple, tea	*Malus hupehensis*
Dogwood, Chinese	*Cornus Kousa*
Dogwood, flowering	*Cornus florida*
Dogwood, giant	*Cornus controversa*
Dove-tree	*Davidia involucrata*

182

Ehretia, heliotrope	*Ehretia thyrsiflora*
Epaulette-tree	*Pterostyrax hispida*
Franklin-tree	*Franklinia alatamaha*
Fringe-tree, Chinese	*Chionanthus retusus*
Fringe-tree, white	*Chionanthus virginicus*
Haw, black-	*Viburnum prunifolium*
Hawthorn, Washington	*Crataegus Phaenopyrum*
Locust, black	*Robinia Pseudoacacia*
Magnolia, anise	*Magnolia salicifolia*
Magnolia, evergreen	*Magnolia grandiflora*
Magnolia, Kobus	*Magnolia Kobus*
Magnolia, Yulan	*Magnolia denudata*
Peach, white, semi-double	*Prunus Persica* 'Alba-plena'
Pear, Callery	*Pyrus Calleryana*
Photinia	*Photinia villosa*
Plum, beach	*Prunus maritima*
Service-berry, smooth	*Amelanchier laevis*
Silverbell, Carolina	*Halesia carolina*
Snowbells	*Styrax* species
Stewartias	*Stewartia* species
Viburnum, Siebold	*Viburnum Sieboldii*
Yellowwood	*Cladrastis lutea*

FRAGRANCE

(* = unpleasant to some people)

Alder, white-	*Clethra barbinervis*
Beebee-tree, Korean	*Evodia Daniellii*
* Cherry, black	*Prunus serotina*
Cherry, Oriental	*Prunus serrulata*

183

FLOWERING TREES

Cherry, Yoshino	*Prunus yedoensis*
* Chestnut, Chinese	*Castanea mollissima*
Crabapple, Arnold	*Malus arnoldiana*
Crabapple, Bechtel	*Malus ioensis* 'Plena'
Crabapple, carmine	*Malus atrosanguinea*
Crabapple, cutleaf	*Malus toringoides*
Crabapple, 'Dorothea'	*Malus* 'Dorothea'
Crabapple, flowering-, Chinese	*Malus spectabilis* 'Riversii'
Crabapple, flowering-, Japanese	*Malus floribunda*
Crabapple, Katherine	*Malus* 'Katherine'
Crabapple, Lemoine	*Malus purpurea* 'Lemoinei'
Crabapple, Parkman	*Malus Halliana* 'Parkmanii'
Crabapple, Sargent	*Malus Sargentii*
Crabapple, Scheidecker	*Malus Scheideckeri*
Crabapple, slender Siberian	*Malus baccata* 'gracilis'
Crabapple, tea	*Malus hupehensis*
Ehretia, heliotrope	*Ehretia thyrsiflora*
Haw, black-	*Viburnum prunifolium*
* Hawthorn, Washington	*Crataegus Phaenopyrum*
Lilac, Japanese	*Syringa amurensis* var. *japonica*
Lilac, Peking	*Syringa pekinensis*
Linden, Crimean	*Tilia euchlora*
Linden, European largeleaf	*Tilia platyphyllos*
Linden, European littleleaf	*Tilia cordata*
Linden, pendent silver	*Tilia petiolaris*
Linden, silver	*Tilia tomentosa*
Locust, black	*Robinia Pseudoacacia*
Maackia	*Maackia chinensis*
* Magnolia, evergreen	*Magnolia grandiflora*
Magnolia, Kobus	*Magnolia Kobus*

184

Magnolia, saucer	*Magnolia Soulangiana*
Magnolia, sweetbay	*Magnolia virginiana*
Magnolia, Yulan	*Magnolia denudata*
Olive, Russian-	*Elaeagnus angustifolia*
Peach	*Prunus Persica*
* Pear, Callery	*Pyrus Calleryana*
* Plum, beach	*Prunus maritima*
Silk-tree, hardy	*Albizia Julibrissin*
	var. *rosea*
Snowbell, fragrant	*Styrax Obassia*
* Viburnum, Siebold	*Viburnum Sieboldii*
Yellowwood	*Cladrastis lutea*

Appendix II: Special Uses for Flowering Trees

Flowering trees, as I noted in the Foreword, will give an outstanding performance in any landscape role—alone or in groups, in formal or informal (naturalistic) plantings. This chapter discusses a number of situations in which certain of these trees may be used. The inexperienced person might hesitate to employ such suggestions. But a landscape designer is always alert to possible new combinations. Amateurs in doubt are advised to consult with a successful practitioner.

Remember that if a flowering tree is to stand alone, perhaps as a lawn specimen, it should have substantial characteristics above and beyond floral attractiveness (see Chapter 3). Handsome foliage and sturdy trunk are usual requisites. The winter aspect ought to be considered: bark, buds and branching pattern are attributes which contribute to the qualifications of a flowering tree as a specimen. Here are a few recommendations:

SPECIMEN FLOWERING TREES

Alder, white-	*Clethra barbinervis*
Ash, mountain-	*Sorbus Aucuparia, S. alnifolia*

186

Catalpa, Chinese	*Catalpa ovata*
Cherries	*Prunus* species
Cherry, cornelian-	*Cornus mas*
Chestnut, Chinese	*Castanea mollissima*
Chestnuts, horse-	*Aesculus* species
Crabapples	*Malus* species
Dogwoods	*Cornus* species
Dove-tree	*Davidia involucrata*
Ehretia, heliotrope	*Ehretia thyrsiflora*
Empress-tree	*Paulownia tomentosa*
Epaulette-tree	*Pterostyrax hispida*
Fringe-trees	*Chionanthus* species
Golden-chain, Waterer's	*Laburnum Watereri*
Goldenrain-tree	*Koelreuteria paniculata*
Idesia	*Idesia polycarpa*
Lilacs	*Syringa* species
Lindens	*Tilia* species
Magnolias	*Magnolia* species
Pear, Callery	*Pyrus Calleryana*
Plums	*Prunus* species
Raisin-tree, Japanese	*Hovenia dulcis*
Scholar-tree, Chinese	*Sophora japonica*
Silk-tree, hardy	*Albizia Julibrissin* var. *rosea*
Silverbell, mountain	*Halesia monticola* 'Rosea'
Smoke-tree	*Cotinus Coggygria*
Sourwood	*Oxydendrum arboreum*
Stewartias	*Stewartia* species
Tulip-tree	*Liriodendron Tulipifera*
Viburnum, Siebold	*Viburnum Sieboldii*
Yellowwood	*Cladrastis lutea*

FLOWERING TREES

AVENUE FLOWERING TREES

Suburban streets, boulevards and long approach roads call for stately treatment. The following flowering trees lend themselves to formality:

	Shade	Stately	Hospitable
Ash, mountain-, Korean (*Sorbus alnifolia*)			x
Catalpa, Chinese (*Catalpa ovata*)	x	x	
Cherry, Oriental (*Prunus serrulata*)			x
Cherry, Sargent (*Prunus Sargentii*)	x		
Cherry, Yoshino (*Prunus yedoensis*)			x
Chestnuts, horse- (*Aesculus* species)	x	x	
Hawthorn, Washington (*Crataegus Phaenopyrum*)			x
Lindens (*Tilia* species)	x	x	
Locust, black (*Robinia Pseudo-acacia*)			x
Magnolia, evergreen (*Magnolia grandiflora*)		x	
Scholar-tree, Chinese (*Sophora japonica*)	x		x
Tulip-tree (*Liriodendron Tulipifera*)	x		
Viburnum, Siebold (*Viburnum Sieboldii*)		x	

GROUP OR GROVE

In parks and along parkways, where groves of similar flowering trees will enhance the setting, the following species are suggested. When the grouping is small, the number of plants ought to be of an odd number, such as three, five, seven, and so on. (Trees that set fruit only with cross-pollination are marked with an asterisk.)

Beebee-tree	*Evodia Daniellii*
Birch, gray	*Betula populifolia*
Cherries	*Prunus* species
Cherry, cornelian-	*Cornus mas*
* Chestnut	*Castanea mollissima*
Crabapples	*Malus* species
Dogwoods	*Cornus* species
* Fringe-trees	*Chionanthus* species
Haw, black-	*Viburnum prunifolium*
* Idesia	*Idesia polycarpa*
Lilacs	*Syringa* species
Locust, black	*Robinia Pseudoacacia*
Magnolias	*Magnolia* species
* Plums	*Prunus,* certain species
Stewartias	*Stewartia* species
Smoke-tree	*Cotinus Coggygria*
* Tree of heaven	*Ailanthus altissima*
Yellowwood	*Cladrastis lutea*

GROUPED WITH EVERGREENS

When variety in landscape scenes is desired, such as on small home grounds, a grouping of several kinds of flowering tree with needled evergreens would be appropriate. Trees from the following list may be combined with pine, hemlock, or other

189

FLOWERING TREES

coniferous plants to create pleasing landscape group compositions:

Alder, white-	*Sorbus Aucuparia*
Ash, mountain-, European	*Betula populifolia*
Birch, gray	*Prunus* species
Cherries	*Cornus mas*
Cherry, cornelian-	*Malus* species
Crabapples	*Cornus* species
Dogwoods	*Ehretia thyrsiflora*
Ehretia, heliotrope	*Pterostyrax hispida*
Epaulette-tree	*Franklinia alatamaha*
Franklin-tree	*Chionanthus* species
Fringe-trees	*Laburnum Watereri*
Golden-chain, Waterer's	*Crataegus Phaenopyrum*
Hawthorn, Washington	*Syringa* species
Lilacs	*Maackia chinensis*
Maackia	*Magnolia* species
Magnolias	*Pyrus Calleryana*
Pear, Callery	*Photinia villosa*
Photinia	*Prunus* species
Plums	*Cercis canadensis*
Redbud	*Amelanchier laevis*
Service-berry, smooth	*Halesia* species
Silverbells	*Oxydendrum arboreum*
Sourwood	*Stewartia* species
Stewartias	*Viburnum Sieboldii*
Viburnum, Siebold	*Clethra barbinervis*

SPECIAL USES FOR FLOWERING TREES

ONE PLUS EVERGREENS

Here is a list of flowering trees, each of whose beauty is enhanced when it is planted against needled evergreens. The intent is to place a single plant in contrast with the evergreen backdrop:

Ash, mountain-, European	*Sorbus Aucuparia*
Ash, mountain-, Korean	*Sorbus alnifolia*
Birch, gray	*Betula populifolia*
Cherries	*Prunus* species
Cherry, cornelian-	*Cornus mas*
Crabapples	*Malus* species
Dogwoods	*Cornus* species
Dove-tree	*Davidia involucrata*
Epaulette-tree	*Pterostyrax hispida*
Franklin-tree	*Franklinia alatamaha*
Fringe-trees	*Chionanthus* species
Golden-chain, Waterer's	*Laburnum Watereri*
Hawthorn, Washington	*Crataegus Phaenopyrum*
Lilacs	*Syringa* species
Magnolias	*Magnolia* species
Olive, Russian-	*Elaeagnus angustifolia*
Pear, Callery	*Pyrus Calleryana*
Plums	*Prunus* species
Redbud	*Cercis canadensis*
Service-berry, smooth	*Amelanchier laevis*
Silk-tree, hardy	*Albizia Julibrissin* var. *rosea*
Silverbells	*Halesia* species
Smoke-tree	*Cotinus Coggygria*
Snowbells	*Styrax* species

FLOWERING TREES

Sourwood	*Oxydendrum arboreum*
Viburnum, Siebold	*Viburnum Sieboldii*

AT WOODS' EDGE

Many flowering trees by nature occur at the edge of woods or in a wood-rimmed clearing. The following list offers some well-known species, plus some that seldom occur in such places naturally but nevertheless deserve to be considered:

Alder, white-	*Clethra barbinervis*
Ash, mountain-, European	*Sorbus Aucuparia*
Beebee-tree	*Evodia Daniellii*
Birch, gray	*Betula populifolia*
Buckthorn, woolly	*Bumelia lanuginosa*
Cherry, black	*Prunus serotina*
Cherry, cornelian-	*Cornus mas*
Dogwoods	*Cornus* species
Empress-tree	*Paulownia tomentosa*
Franklin-tree	*Franklinia alatamaha*
Fringe-trees	*Chionanthus* species
Haw, black-	*Viburnum prunifolium*
Hawthorn, Washington	*Crataegus Phaenopyrum*
Maackia	*Maackia chinensis*
Photinia	*Photinia villosa*
Redbud	*Cercis canadensis*
Service-berry, smooth	*Amelanchier laevis*
Silverbells	*Halesia* species
Sourwood	*Oxydendrum arboreum*
Tree of heaven	*Ailanthus altissima*

SPECIAL USES FOR FLOWERING TREES

FOR STREET AND PARK

Flowering trees grown for use along streets must have well-developed trunks to allow for pedestrian and vehicular traffic. Along sidewalks the trunks are pruned clean of branches to a height of seven feet, so that even tall persons may walk beneath their branches. But for street use, where trucks are permitted, the branches must all be removed to a height of twelve feet or more.

Straight stems are especially desired although minor crooks may be permitted since, as the trunk enlarges in girth, the irregularities usually are eliminated. In planting young trees along streets be sure to provide a guy-wire and stake set-up for the first few years in order to afford the roots opportunity to become established and also to protect the new tree against injury. In many municipalities throughout the country, streetside tree planting is under the jurisdiction of shade tree commissions. Property owners would do well to seek advice and consent before making such plantings.

Dozens of species of flowering trees have furrowed or rough scaly bark that makes them well suited for street use. Sugar maple, linden, horse-chestnut, Callery pear and scholar-tree are but a few examples of trees with tough bark which will remain attractive despite carvings and other forms of public indifference.

Appendix III: Sequence of Bloom

1st week	2nd week	3rd week	4th week
		APRIL (OR LATE MARCH)	
Cherry, cornelian-	Cherry, rosebud	Cherry, Fuji	Ash, mountain-, European
Plum, purple-leaved	Magnolia, anise	Cherry, Sargent	Ash, mountain-, Korean
	Magnolia, Kobus	Cherry, Yoshino	Birch, gray
	Magnolia, saucer	Peach	Cherry, Oriental
	Magnolia, Yulan	Pear, Callery	Crabapple, Arnold
		Service-berry, smooth	Crabapple, carmine
			Crabapple, Dorothea
			Crabapple, flowering-, Chinese
			Crabapple, flowering-, Japanese
			Crabapple, Katherine
			Crabapple, Lemoine
			Crabapple, Parkman
			Crabapple, Scheidecker
			Crabapple, slender Siberian
			Crabapple, tea
			Dogwood, flowering
			Haw, black-
			Pear, Callery
			Plum, beach
			Redbud

MAY

Crabapple, Bechtel
Crabapple, cutleaf
Crabapple, Sargent
Dove-tree
Silverbell, Carolina
Silverbell, mountain

Buckeye, sweet
Chestnut, horse-, double
Chestnut, horse-, ruby
Empress-tree
Viburnum, Siebold

Cherry, black
Golden-chain, Waterer's
Photinia
Snowbell, fragrant
Snowbell, Japanese

Dogwood, Chinese
Dogwood, giant
Fringe-tree, Chinese
Fringe-tree, white
Locust, black
Magnolia, sweetbay
Tulip-tree

JUNE

Hawthorn, Washington
Idesia
Lilac, tree, Japanese
Olive, Russian-
Yellowwood

Catalpa, Chinese
Chestnut, Chinese
Ehretia, heliotrope
Epaulette-tree
Linden, European largeleaf
Smoke-tree

Lilac, Peking
Linden, Crimean
Linden, pendent silver
Linden, silver
Magnolia, evergreen
Stewartia, Japanese
Stewartia, Korean
Tree of heaven

Linden, European little-leaf
Raisin-tree, Japanese
Silk-tree, hardy

JULY

Goldenrain-tree

Beebee-tree, Korean
Maackia
Sourwood

Alder, white-, Japanese
Scholar-tree, Chinese

AUGUST

Buckthorn, woolly

Franklin-tree

Appendix IV: Flower Identification Table

For explanations of certain words and symbols used here, see "Tree Terms to Know," Appendix IX. Letters under Fertility are: D = dioecious, F = fertile, M = monoecious, N = sterile. Under Position on Stem: C = flower borne on current season's growth; Mx = flower and foliage borne from same bud; O = flower borne on old wood, a branchlet of previous season; l = lateral or axillary, t = terminal on spur or lateral shoot, tt = terminal on new shoot. Under Time: a = after the leaves have unfolded, b = before the leaves appear, w = expanding as leaves are unfolding. Under Size: * indicates the size of a single flower.

Common Name	Scientific Name	Fertility	Type	Position on Stem	Time of Bloom	Number of flowers in each cluster	Flower size in inches
Aesculus, see Buckeye; Chestnut, horse-							
Ailanthus, see Tree of heaven							
Albizia, see Silk-tree							
Alder, white, Japanese	Clethra barbinervis	F	raceme	Ctt	a	many	4-6 long
Amelanchier, see Service-berry							

Common name	Scientific name		Inflorescence				Size
Ash, mountain-, European	Sorbus Aucuparia	F	corymb	Ctl	b	8-10	4-6 across
Ash, mountain-, Korean	Sorbus alnifolia	F	corymb	Ctl	w	6-10	1-½ across
Beebee-tree, Korean	Evodia Daniellii	D	cyme	Mxt	a	many	4-6 across
Betula, see Birch							
Birch, gray	Betula populifolia	M	catkin	Ol	w	many	3-4 long
Buckeye, sweet	Aesculus octandra	F	thyrse	Mxt	a	many	4-6 long
Buckthorn, woolly	Bumelia lanuginosa	F	fascicle	Mxl	a	many	1-1¼ across
Bumelia, see Buckthorn							
Castanea, see Chestnut							
Catalpa, Chinese	Catalpa ovata	F	cyme	Mxt	a	many	8-12 long
Cercis, see Redbud							
Cherry, black	Prunus serotina	F	raceme	Ctl	w	many	4-6 long
Cherry, cornelian-	Cornus mas	F	fascicle	Otl	b	many	1-1½ across
Cherry, Fuji	Prunus incisa	F	raceme	Ol	b	1-few	* ¾-1 across
Cherry, Oriental	Prunus serrulata	N	raceme	Ol	b	3-5	* 1-1½ across
Cherry, rosebud	Prunus subhirtella var. pendula	F	raceme	Ol	b	2-5	* 1 across
Cherry, Sargent	Prunus Sargentii	F	umbel	Ol	b	2-4	* 1-1½ across
Cherry, Yoshino	Prunus yedoensis	F	raceme	Ol	b	5-6	* 1-1½ across
Chestnut, Chinese	Castanea mollissima	M	catkin	Mxl	a	many	6-8 long

Common Name	Scientific Name	Fertility	Type	Position on Stem	Time of Bloom	Number of flowers in each cluster	Flower size in inches
Chestnut, horse-, double	Aesculus Hippocastanum 'Baumannii'	N	thyrse	Mxt	a	many	8-12 long
Chestnut, horse-, ruby	Aesculus carnea 'Briotii'	F	thyrse	Mxt	a	many	5-12 long
Chioanthus, see Fringe-tree							
Cladrastis, see Yellowwood							
Clethra, see Alder, white-							
Cornus, see Dogwood							
Cotinus, see Smoke-tree							
Crabapple, Arnold	Malus arnoldiana	F	cyme	Otl	b	7	* 1¼-1½ across
Crabapple, Bechtel	Malus ioensis 'Plena'	N	cyme	Otl	a	7	* 1½-2 across
Crabapple, carmine	Malus atrosanguinea	F	cyme	Otl	b	7	* 1-1¼ across
Crabapple, cutleaf	Malus toringoides	F	cyme	Otl	a	7	* ¾-1 across
Crabapple, Dorothea	Malus 'Dorothea'	F	cyme	Otl	b	7	* 1½-2 across
Crabapple, flowering-, Chinese	Malus spectabilis 'Riversii'	N	cyme	Otl	b	7	* 1½-2 across
Crabapple, flowering-, Japanese	Malus floribunda	F	cyme	Otl	b	7	* 1-1¼ across
Crabapple, Katherine	Malus 'Katherine'	F	cyme	Otl	b	7	* 1½-2 across

Common name	Scientific name		Inflorescence		Color	Number	Size
Crabapple, Lemoine	*Malus purpurea* 'Lemoinei'	F	cyme	Otl	w	7	* 1-1½ across
Crabapple, Parkman	*Malus Halliana* 'Parkmanii'	N	cyme	Otl	b	7	* 1¼-1½ across
Crabapple, Sargent	*Malus Sargentii*	F	cyme	Otl	a	7	* 1 across
Crabapple, Scheidecker	*Malus Scheideckeri*	F	cyme	Otl	b	7	* 1¼-1½ across
Crabapple, slender Siberian	*Malus baccata* 'Gracilis'	F	cyme	Otl	w	7	* 1¼-1½ across
Crabapple, tea	*Malus hupehensis*	F	cyme	Otl	b	7	* 1½ across
Crateagus, see Hawthorn							
Davidia, see Dove-tree							
Dogwood, Chinese	*Cornus Kousa*	F	glomerule	Otl	a	many	2-4 across
Dogwood, flowering	*Cornus florida*	F	glomerule	Otl	b	many	3-4 across
Dogwood, giant *see also* Cherry cornelian-	*Cornus controversa*	F	corymb	Otl	a	many	2½-5 across
Dove-tree	*Davidia involucrata*	F	head	Otl	w	1-many	6½ long
Ehretia, heliotrope	*Ehretia thyrsiflora*	F	thyrse	Mxt	a	many	3-8 long
Elaeagnus, see Olive, Russian-							
Empress-tree	*Paulownia tomentosa*	F	panicle	Otl	b	many	8-12 long
Epaulette-tree	*Pterostyrax hispida*	F	raceme	Otl	a	many	5-10 long
Evodia, see Beebee-tree							

199

Common Name	Scientific Name	Fertility	Type	Position on Stem	Time of Bloom	Number of flowers in each cluster	Flower size in inches
Franklin-tree	Franklinia alatamaha	F	solitary	Cl	a	1	* 3 across
Fringe-tree, Chinese	Chionanthus retusus	D	cyme	Mxt	w	many	2½-4 long
Fringe-tree, white	Chionanthus virginicus	D	cyme	Mxl	w	many	4-8 long
Golden-chain, Water-er's	Laburnum Watereri	F	raceme	Mxt	b	many	12 long
Goldenrain-tree	Koelreuteria paniculata	F	raceme	Mxt	a	many	14 long
Halesia, see Silver-bell							
Haw, black-	Viburnum prunifolium	F	cyme	Otl	w	many	2-4 across
Hawthorn, Washing-ton	Crataegus Phaenopyrum	F	corymb	Otl	a	many	1½-2 across
Horse-chestnut, see Chestnut, horse-							
Hovenia, see Raisin-tree							
Idesia	Idesia polycarpa	D	cyme	Mxt	a	many	4-10 long
Koelreuteria, see Goldenrain-tree							
Laburnum, see Golden-chain							
Lilac, Peking	Syringa pekinensis	F	thyrse	Ot	a	many	3-6 long
Lilac, tree., Japanese	Syringa amurensis var. japonica	F	thyrse	Ot	a	many	4-6 long
Linden, Crimean	Tilia euchlora	F	cyme	Mxl	a	3-7	2-3 long

Common name	Species		Inflorescence	Position		Number	Size
Linden, European largeleaf	Tilia platyphyllos	F	cyme	Mxl	a	3-6	2-6 long
Linden, European littleleaf	Tilia cordata	F	cyme	Mxl	a	5-7	¾-1½ long
Linden, pendent silver	Tilia petiolaris	F	cyme	Mxl	a	3-10	1-2½ long
Linden, silver	Tilia tomentosa	F	cyme	Mxl	a	7-10	1-1½ long
Liriodendron, see Tulip-tree							
Locust, black	Robinia Pseudoacacia	F	raceme	Mxt	b	many	4-8 long
Maackia	Maackia chinensis	F	raceme	Mxt	a	many	4-8 long
Magnolia, anise	Magnolia salicifolia	F	solitary	Otl	b	1	* across
Magnolia, evergreen	Magnolia grandiflora	F	solitary	Ctl	a	1	* 7-8 across
Magnolia, Kobus	Magnolia Kobus	F	solitary	Otl	b	1	* 4-5 across
Magnolia, saucer	Magnolia Soulangiana	F	solitary	Otl	b	1	* 4-6 across
Magnolia, sweetbay	Magnolia virginiana	F	solitary	Ctl	a	1	* 2-3 across
Magnolia, Yulan	Magnolia denudata	F	solitary	Otl	b	1	* 5-6 across
Malus, see Crabapple							
Mountain-ash, see Ash, mountain-							
Oleander, see Olive, Russian-							
Olive, Russian-	Elaeagnus angustifolia	F	solitary	Mxl	a	1	* ½ long
Oxydendrum, see Sourwood							
Paulownia, see Empress-tree							

Common Name	Scientific Name	Fertility	Type	Position on Stem	Time of Bloom	Number of flowers in each cluster	Flower size in inches
Peach	Prunus Persica	N	solitary	Ol	b	1	* 2 across
Pear, Atsuki-, see Ash, mountain-, Korean							
Pear, Callery	Pyrus Calleryana	F	cyme	Otl	b	few	2-2½ across
Photinia	Photinia villosa	F	corymb	Ctl	a	many	1-1½ across
Plum, beach	Prunus maritima	D	umbel	Ol	b	many	¾-1¼ across
Plum, purple-leaved	Prunus cerasifera 'Pissardii'	F	umbel	Ol	b	1-3	1 across
Prunus, see Cherry; Peach; Plum							
Pterostyrax, see Epaulette-tree							
Pyrus, see Pear, Callery							
Raisin-tree, Japanese	Hovenia dulcis	F	cyme	Mxl	a	many	1½-2½ across
Redbud	Cercis canadensis	F	fascicle	Ol	b	4-8	¾-1½ across
Robinia, see Locust							
Russian-olive, see Olive, Russian-							
Scholar-tree, Chinese	Sophora japonica	F	panicle	Ctt	a	many	6-12 long
Service-berry, smooth	Amelanchier laevis	F	raceme	Mxt	b	many	1¼-2 long
Silk-tree, hardy	Albizia Julibrissin var. rosea	F	head	Ctt	a	many	1-1½ across

Common name	Botanical name						
Silverbell, Carolina	*Halesia carolina*	F	cyme	Otl	b	2-5	1½ long
Silverbell, mountain	*Halesia monticola* 'Rosea'	F	cyme	Otl	b	2-5	2 long
Smoke-tree	*Cotinus Coggygria*	F	cyme	Mxt	a	many	6-8 long
Snowbell, fragrant	*Styrax Obassia*	F	raceme	Otl	a	many	4-8 long
Snowbell, Japanese	*Styrax japonica*	F	raceme	Otl	a	3-6	1-1½ long
Sophora, see Scholar-tree							
Sorbus, see Ash, mountain-							
Sourwood	*Oxydendrum arboreum*	F	raceme	Ctt	a	many	4-6 long
Stewartia, Japanese	*Stewartia Pseudo-Camellia*	F	solitary	Mxl	a	1	* 2-2½ across
Stewartia, Korean	*Stewartia koreana*	F	solitary	Mxl	a	1	* 3 across
Styrax, see Snowbell							
Syringa, see Lilac							
Tilia, see Linden							
Tree of heaven	*Ailanthus altissima*	D	panicle	Mxt	a	many	4-8 long
Tulip-tree	*Liriodendron Tulipifera*	F	solitary	Ctl	a	1	* 2-2½ across
Viburnum prunifolium, see Haw, black-							
Viburnum, Siebold	*Viburnum Sieboldii*	F	cyme	Otl	a	many	3-4 across
Yellowwood	*Cladrastis lutea*	F	raceme	Mxt	a	many	10-16 long

203

Appendix V: Flowering Trees with Fleshy Fruits

RED FRUITS

Tree	Month of ripening
Cherry, cornelian-	— July
Crabapple, carmine	— September
Crabapple, cutleaf	— September
Crabapple, slender Siberian	— September
Dogwood, Chinese	— August
Dogwood, flowering	— September
Haw, black- (pink in ripening)	— August
Magnolias (seed covering)	— September
Ash, mountain-, Korean	— September
Photinia	— September
Plum, beach	— September

ORANGE

Ash, mountain-, European	— August
Hawthorn, Washington	— September
Idesia	— September

FLOWERING TREES WITH FLESHY FRUITS

Tree	*Month of ripening*
Pear, Callery	— October
Raisin-tree	— September

YELLOW

Crabapple, Arnold	— September
Crabapple, carmine	— September
Crabapple, cutleaf	— September
Crabapple, Dorothea	— September
Crabapple, flowering-, Japanese	— September
Crabapple, Katherine	— September
Crabapple, Scheidecker	— September
Crabapple, tea	— September
Magnolias (fruit cones)	— September
Scholar-tree, Chinese	— October

SILVERY

Olive, Russian-	— September

BLUE

Fringe-trees	— September

PURPLE

Crabapple, Lemoine	— September
Crabapple, Parkman	— September
Crabapple, Sargent	— September
Plum, beach	— September
Plum, purple-leaved	— July
Service-berry	— June
Smoke-tree	— June

FLOWERING TREES

BLUE- OR PURPLE-BLACK

Tree		Month of ripening
Buckthorn, woolly	—	October
Cherries, ornamental	—	Steptember
Dogwood, giant	—	August
Haw, black-	—	September
Viburnum, Siebold	—	July

Appendix VI: Flowering Trees—Autumn Foliage

YELLOW

Alder, white-	*Clethra barbinervis*
Beebee-tree	*Evodia Daniellii*
Birch, gray	*Betula populifolia*
Chestnut, Chinese	*Castanea mollissima*
Fringe-trees	*Chionanthus* species
Goldenrain-tree	*Koelreuteria paniculata*
Magnolia, sweetbay	*Magnolia virginiana*
Redbud	*Cercis canadensis*
Scholar-tree, Chinese	*Sophora japonica*
Silverbells	*Halesia* species
Tree of heaven	*Ailanthus altissima*
Tulip-tree	*Liriodendron Tulipifera*
Yellowwood	*Cladrastis lutea*

RED-PURPLE SHADES

Ash, mountain-, Korean	*Sorbus alnifolia*
Cherry, black	*Prunus serotina*

FLOWERING TREES

Cherry, cornelian-	*Cornus mas*
Cherry, Oriental	*Prunus serrulata*
Cherry, Sargent	*Prunus Sargentii*
Crabapple, cutleaf	*Malus toringoides*
Dogwoods	*Cornus* species
Ehretia, heliotrope	*Ehretia thyrsiflora*
Franklin-tree	*Franklinia alatamaha*
Haw, black-	*Viburnum prunifolium*
Hawthorn, Washington	*Crataegus Phaenopyrum*
Pear, Callery	*Pyrus Calleryana*
Photinia	*Photinia villosa*
Plum, beach	*Prunus maritima*
Service-berry, smooth	*Amelanchier laevis*
Smoke-tree	*Cotinus Coggygria*
Sourwood	*Oxydendrum arboreum*
Stewartias	*Stewartia* species

Appendix VII: Forcing Branches

Local and major spring flower shows scheduled for late winter or very early spring present a special problem in that branches or plants must be in bloom at a particular date. They must be forced into bloom ahead of their normal time. Even professional gardeners sometimes miss a show's opening day. With all the things that can go wrong, it is a wonder how anyone succeeds in estimating correctly just when to bring specimens indoors or into a greenhouse for forcing.

The closer the show's opening date to the tree's normal blooming period, the shorter the period required for forcing. With forsythia, for example, once the flower buds have begun to swell on the plant's branches in late March, it takes only a day or so to have flowers fully opened after you have cut the branches and put them into containers of water indoors. On the other hand, a crabapple branch cut and brought in at the same time will take much longer to bloom. Also with any tree, the larger the branch the longer the forcing time and the more alteration of the tree's form. However, flowers on these large branches usually last longer. A complete small-sized young tree, with roots balled and burlaped, can be forced into bloom in about the same amount of time as a large branch cut from an older specimen. Of course, if you have only saplings on your property, you had best forget about forcing branches for a few years.

Flower buds and leaf buds for forcing are borne on branchlets of last year. There may also be mixed buds containing embryo leaves and flowers in one "package." In any case they only await favorable conditions for blooming. This indicates that greater success will be achieved by selecting those flowering trees which normally are early blooming. The following is a list of possible forcing subjects, adapted from studies by Dr. Donald Wyman of the Arnold Arboretum. The list gives suggested dates for bringing balled and burlapped trees or large branches indoors for forcing to meet a flower-show opening date of March fifteenth. It also cites each tree's flowering time. Remember that for best results night temperatures should not fall much below 60 degrees F.

Greenhouse and indoor space is at a premium during the winter. Nevertheless, it is wise to force more material than you expect to need in the show. In addition to quantity "insurance," this system gives you a chance to be selective, so that only the choicest material will be placed on exhibition.

Of course, branches obtained as a result of dormant pruning may be brought into the house and forced into bloom for your own enjoyment. Pussywillows are favorites for winter bouquets. Other catkin-bearing trees are best avoided, since the pollen may scatter on table and carpet.

210

Type of Flowering Symbol Key:
* uncertain results for effort; Mx = mixed bud; O = blooming
on previous year's wood; l = lateral; t = terminal.

Bring Inside not later than	Tree	Normal Flowering period	Type of flowering
Jan. 1*	Fringe-tree	May 4th week	Mx
Jan. 1*	Dogwood, Chinese	May 4th week	Otl
Jan. 10*	Snowbell, Japanese	May 3rd week	Otl
Jan. 10*	Golden-chain, Waterer's	May 3rd week	Mxt
Jan. 20*	Chestnut, horse-	May 2nd week	Mxt
Jan. 20*	Empress-tree	May 2nd week	Otl
Jan. 30	Silverbell, mountain	May 1st week	Otl
Jan. 29	Dogwood, flowering	Apr. 4th week	Otl
Feb. 5	Crabapples	Apr. 4th week	Otl
Feb. 18	Redbud	Apr. 4th week	Ol
Feb. 10	Cherry, Oriental (double)	Apr. 4th week	Ol
Feb. 22	Cherry, Sargent	Apr. 3rd week	Ol
Feb. 23	Cherry, Yoshino	Apr. 3rd week	Ol
Mar. 5-8	Cherry, Fuji	Apr. 3rd week	Ol
Mar. 5-8	Cherry, rosebud	Apr. 2nd week	Ol
Mar. 5-8	Magnolia, saucer	Apr. 2nd week	Otl
few days prior	Plum, purple-leaf	Apr. 1st week	Ol
day or so prior	Cherry, cornelian-	Mar. 4th week	Otl

211

Appendix VIII: Where to See Flowering Trees

More than one hundred collections of trees are to be found from Maine to California and across Canada. These are growing in botanical gardens, arboretums, campuses, cemeteries, parks, nurseries, and estates that have been oriented for public benefit. The listing in this chapter includes only those institutions or gardens open to the public. Few if any of these collections are complete, but they do have invaluable representation of trees that are adapted to the peculiarities of the climate, soil and other conditions in their locality.

The list of places is arranged according to regions with similar climates. Thus, it may at first seem strange that I have included a southern city with some northern cities, as in the case of Asheville, North Carolina, being in the same category with Boston, but this is a more logical approach than the political grouping of states. Likewise, Spokane, situated in the "inland Empire" and having a climate somewhat similar to that of Los Angeles and Denver, is included in the Southwestern province, even though geographically it would seem to belong to the Pacific Northwest.

There are five divisions recognized in this climate-group treatment: Northeastern, Southeastern, Middle Western, Southwestern and Pacific Northwestern. Omitted are the plains, mountains and subtropical portions of Florida, Texas and California. Since the book's emphasis is on hardy trees, the subtropical sections are necessarily excluded. So are trees of the plains, where rainfall is generally too scant to support extensive natural growth of trees (unless they are irrigated and protected by screens).

The Value of an Arboretum

By definition an arboretum is a collection of trees. The development of an arboretum chiefly depends upon the means and management of the owner. Traditionally, kings have had hunting parks, queens and nobles their gardens. Today when everyone is king, we wish our grounds suitably embellished. How may we decide upon which trees to plant? Narratives of history or travel may kindle desires for certain plants, but seeing the actual plant is the strongest incentive for wishing to have such a specimen in one's own landscape.

Opportunities to see flowering trees are innumerable. A wide variety of parks and gardens, public and private, are open to visitors. Each region of the country provides at least one place for observing plant materials. In order to be useful for study, the collection must have its plants labeled or otherwise identified so that further investigation can be made regarding uses of the plant, rate of growth, soil and water requirements and so on.

Here is a list of arboretums, botanical gardens, public gardens and parks, cited according to climate groups:

213

FLOWERING TREES

NORTHEAST

Quebec:
Montreal Botanical Gerden, 4101 Sherbrooke St. East, Montreal.

Morgan Arboretum, Macdonald College, McGill University, Montreal.

Ontario:
Dominion Arboretum and Botanic Garden, Science Service Bldg., Carling Ave., Ottawa.

Maine:
Botanical Plantations of the University of Maine, 203 Deering Hall, Orono.

Massachusetts:
Arnold Arboretum, Harvard University, Jamaica Plain 30.

Berkshire Garden Center, Stockbridge.
Botanic Garden of Smith College, Northhampton.

Alexandra Botanic Garden and Hunnewell Arboretum, Wellesley College, Wellesley.

Connecticut:
Marsh Botanic Garden, Yale University, New Haven.

Connecticut Arboretum, Connecticut College, New London.

New York:
Brooklyn Botanic Garden, 1000 Washington Ave., Brooklyn 25.

George Landis Arboretum, Esperance.

Thomas C. Desmond Arboretum, Newburgh.

New York Botanical Garden, Bronx Park, New York 58.

Planting Fields Arboretum, Oyster Bay, Long Island.

New Jersey:

Rutgers Display Gardens, New Jersey. Agricultural Experiment Station, New Brunswick.

Cedar Brook Park, Union County Park Commission, Plainfield.

Willowwood Arboretum, Gladstone.

Phillipsburg High School Arboretum, Phillipsburg.

Pennsylvania:

Taylor Memorial Arboretum, 10 Ridley Dr., Garden City, Chester.

Masonic Homes Arboretum, Elizabethtown.

Longwood Gardens, Kennett Square.

John J. Tyler Arboretum, Lima, Delaware Co.

Mont Alto State Forest Arboretum, Mont Alto.

Ellis School Arboretum, Newton Square.

Morris Arboretum, University of Pennsylvania, 9414 Meadowbrook Lane., Philadelphia 18.

Botanical Garden, Reading Public Museum and Art Gallery, 500 Museum Road, Reading.

Arthur Hoyt Scott Horticultural Foundation, Swarthmore College, Swarthmore.

Bowman's Hill Wild Flower Preserve, Washington Crossing State Park, Washington Crossing.

Westtown School Arboretum, Westtown.

Delaware: Henry Francis duPont Winterthur Arboretum, Winterthur.

District of Columbia: United States National Arboretum, 1600 Bladensburg Road, N.E., Washington 2.

Virginia: Orland E. White Arboretum, Boyce.

Virginia Polytechnical Institute Arboretum, Department of Horticulture, Blacksburg.

West Virginia: West Virginia University Arboretum, Morgantown.

North Carolina: Biltmore Estate Arboretum, Biltmore Station, Asheville.

SOUTHEAST

Virginia:	Norfolk Botanic Garden, Norfolk. Marymount Park, Richmond.
North Carolina:	Coker Arboretum, University of North Carolina, Chapel Hill.
	Sarah P. Duke Memorial Garden, Duke University, Durham.
South Carolina:	Magnolia Gardens, Route 2, Johns Island, Charleston.
	Brookgreen Gardens, Georgetown.
Georgia:	Ida Cason Calloway Gardens, Pine Mountain.
Florida:	Wilmot Memorial Garden, University of Florida, Gainsville.
Tennessee:	Southwestern Arboretum, Biology Department, Southwestern College, Memphis.
	W. C. Paul Arboretum, Audubon Park, 800 South Cherry Road, Memphis.

MIDDLE WEST

Ontario:	Royal Botanical Gardens, Hamilton.
	Gardening School Arboretum, Niagara Parks Commission, Niagara Falls.

217

FLOWERING TREES

New York:
Cornell Plantations, Cornell University, Ithaca.

Highland and Durand-Eastman Parks, 5 Castle Park, Rochester 20.

Ohio:
Mt. Airy Arboretum, Cincinnati Park Board, 950 Eden Park Drive, Cincinnati 2.

Stanley M. Rowe Arboretum, 4500 Muchmore Road, Cincinnati.

Kingwood Center, 900 Park Ave. West, Mansfield.

Holden Arboretum, Mentor.

Dawes Arboretum, Newark.

Secrest Arboretum, Agricultural Experiment Station, Wooster.

Kentucky:
General Electric Appliance Park, Louisville.

Indiana:
James Irving Holcomb Botanic Gardens, Butler University, 46th & Sunset Sts., Indianapolis.

Illinois:
Morton Arboretum, Lisle.

Michigan:
Nichols Arboretum, 1827 Geddes Avenue, Ann Arbor.

Beal-Garfield Botanic Garden, Michigan State University, South Campus, East Lansing.

Slayton Arboretum, Hillsdale College, Hillsdale.

Wisconsin: Alfred L. Boerner Botanical Garden, Whitenall Park, Hales Corner.

University of Wisconsin Arboretum, Department of Horticulture, Madison.

Paine Art Center and Arboretum, 800 Algona Blvd., Oshkosh.

Minnesota: Hormel Foundation Arboretum, Austin.

Eloise Butler Wild Flower Garden, Theodore Wirth Park, Minneapolis 12.

University of Minnesota Landscape Arboretum, at Excelsior, Horticulture Department, St. Paul 1.

Manitoba: Canada Experimental Farm, Morden

Missouri: Missouri Botanical Garden (Shaw's Garden) in St. Louis; Arboretum in Gray Summit.

Nebraska: Arbor Lodge State Park Arboretum, Nebraska City.

SOUTHWEST

Colorado: Denver Botanical Garden, City Park, 900 York Avenue, Denver.

FLOWERING TREES

Texas:

Forth Worth Botanic Garden, 3220 Botanic Garden Dr., Forth Worth.

Texas A & M College Arboretum and Trial Grounds, College Station.

Arizona:

Boyce Thompson Southwestern Arboretum, Superior.

California:

Los Angeles State and County Arboretum, 301 N. Baldwin Ave., Arcadia.

Regional Parks Botanic Garden, Tilden Regional Park, Berkeley.

University of California Botanical Garden, Berkeley.

Rancho Santa Ana Botanic Garden, 1500 N. College Ave., Claremont.

University of California Arboretum, Davis.

Descanso Gardens, 1418 Descanso Dr., La Canada.

Botanical Garden, University of California, 405 Hilgard Ave., Los Angeles.

Strybing Arboretum and Botanic Garden, Golden Gate Park, San Francisco.

Huntington Botanical Garden, San Marino.

WHERE TO SEE FLOWERING TREES

	Santa Barbara Botanic Garden, 1212 Mission Canyon Rd., Santa Barbara.
	Saratoga Horticultural Foundation, Verde Vista Ln., Saratoga.
Washington:	Finch Arboretum, W. 3404 Woodland Blvd., Spokane.

PACIFIC NORTHWEST

Oregon:	Hoyt Arboretum, 4000 S. W. Fairview Blvd., Portland.
Washington:	University of Washington Arboretum, Seattle 5.
British Columbia:	Queen Elizabeth Arboretum, Stanley Park, 30th Ave. & Cambie St., Vancouver.

Appendix IX: Tree Terms To Know

ALTERNATE, one after another, as leaves occurring singly along a stem.

ANTHER, the pollen-bearing part of the stamen usually borne at the tip of the filament.

ANTHESIS, flowering, or blooming, especially when pollen is shedding, but also denoting the entire flowering period.

ANTHOCYANINS, blue, red, and purple pigments of plants.

ARBORESCENT, attaining the size or habit of a tree.

AXIL, the upper angle formed by a leaf with the stem.

AXILLARY, situated in the axil.

AXIS, the central line of development of a plant, e.g., the main stem.

BACTERIA (plural), microscopic organisms, frequently the carriers of disease in plants, the agents of fermentation, of conversion of dead organic matter into soluble plant nutrients, and of fixation of atmospheric nitrogen in the root tubercles of certain leguminous plants.

BALLED AND BURLAPPED (B & B), the method of handling plants difficult to transplant whereby the roots are dug with soil intact and then the whole is wrapped in burlap.

BERRY, a fleshy or pulpy fruit bearing few to many seeds.

BIPINNATE, twice pinnate, when the divisions of a pinnate leaf are themselves pinnately divided.

BLADE, the expanded portion of a leaf or petal.

BLOOM, the bluish or whitish waxy covering on the surface of many leaves and fruits, e.g., on plum, grape, cabbage leaf, blue spruce needle, etc.

BLOSSOM, the flower.

BOLE, the trunk or stem of a tree.

BRACT, a modified leaf, especially the small or scale-like appendages in a flower cluster, but sometimes large and brightly colored.

BRISTLE, a stiff hair.

BUD, a structure covered with scales or hairs and containing rudimentary leaves and flowers. Buds vary according to type: *vegetative buds* develop into shoots; *flower buds* develop into the inflorescence, *mixed buds* develop both flowers and foliage; buds are further classified by position: *axillary* (lateral) *buds* arise along the stem while *terminal buds* are borne on the summit of the branchlet.

BUD-SCALE, the thin, usually dry, closely folded modified leaf or bract, that serves to protect a bud before expansion.

CALYX, the outer envelope of the flower; collectively the sepals.

CANOPY, the umbrella of foliage.

CAPSULE, a dry, splitting fruit composed of more than one carpel; a pod.

CARPEL, a simple pistil, or one section of a compound pistil, answering to one leaf.

CATALYST, a substance which is responsible for accelerating a chemical reaction and which may be recovered practically unchanged at the end of the process.

CATKIN, a deciduous spike of unisexual flowers without petals, e.g., the male inflorescence of willow, birch, oak, etc.

CHLOROPHYLL, literally green leaf, actually the substance responsible for trapping radiant energy in the conversion of water and carbon dioxide into sugar; that which produces the prevalent green hue of the vegetable kingdom.

CLONE, a collective name for identical individual plants reproduced vegetatively from a single original plant.

COMPLETE, (also called "perfect"), a flower that possesses all the necessary male and female parts so it can pollinate itself. *See also* DIOECIOUS and MONOECIOUS.

COMPOUND, composed of two or more similar but separate parts aggregated into a common whole, e.g., palmately compound leaf of horse-chestnut, trifoliolate compound leaf of poison ivy, pinnately compound leaf of locust, bipinnately compound leaf of silk-tree.

CONE, the often conical, dry, compound fruit consisting of numerous overlapping scales disposed symmetrically around a central axis and bearing seeds; a strobile, as in pines, spruces, firs, etc.

CONICAL, broadly spire-like.

CONIFEROUS, literally cone-bearing, pertaining to members of the pine family.

COROLLA, the inner series of the floral envelopes collectively; actually the petals.

CORYMB, a convex or flat-topped flower cluster whose outer blooms open earlier.

CROSS, a hybrid of any description.

CROSS-POLLINATION, pollen from a flower on one plant fertilizing a flower on another plant.

CROWN (forestry), the canopy of a tree consisting of branches and leaves; also in horticulture, that part of the stem of a herbaccous perennial or seedling at the ground level.

CURRENT SEASON'S (new) WOOD, the shoot growth that developed during the current growing season.

CUTTING, a severed shoot used in vegetative propagation.

CYME, a convex or flat flower cluster whose central blooms open earlier.

DECIDUOUS, falling at end of one season, as leaves of non-evergreen trees.

DEHISCENCE, the process of opening of a capsule or pod.

DIOECIOUS, literally in two houses,. therefore referring to a species whose male and female flowers occur on separate plants, as in the holly. Fruit is produced by female flowers; a male plant must be growing nearby to supply the pollen. *See also* COMPLETE and MONOECIOUS.

DORMANT, literally sleeping, applied to buds before expansion or to the plant itself especially in winter.

DOUBLE-FLOWERING, said of flowers when the number of petals is increased at the expense of other essential organs.

DRUPE, a fleshy non-splitting fruit with a bony, usually one-seeded endocarp; as the cherry or plum.

ELLIPTIC, narrowing to symmetrical rounded ends.

EMBRYO, the rudimentary plantlet within the seed.

ESPALIER, a method of training woody plants against a wall or lattice—a great space saver.

EVERGREEN, a plant that remains green throughout the year. Pines and junipers are examples of narrow-leaved or needled evergreens; rhododrendron and pieris are typical broadleaved evergreens. New leaves are produced every spring. The older leaves do not live and stay green forever; some drop after two or three years, some after four years, but enough leaves remain green on the plant at all times to keep it "evergreen."

FAMILY, a group of related plants on the level above that of genus.

FASTIGIATE, said of a tree whose branches are erect and parallel to the main stem, as Lombardy poplar.

FEATHERED, plumed.

FERTILIZATION, *see* POLLINATION.

FILAMENT, the stalk of the anther.

FILLER PLANT, a rapidly-growing (and usually short-lived) plant used temporarily to occupy a vacant place among slower-developing permanent plants.

FLORET, a single diminutive flower of a compact cluster of flowers.

FORM, a sub-division of a variety or species differing in a single character and usually perpetuated vegetatively.

FRUIT, the seed-bearing product of a plant; the ripened ovary.

FUNGICIDE, a substance used to kill or prevent the activity of a fungus.

FUNGUS, belonging to a class of plants devoid of chlorophyll which perform the function (among others) of reducing organic matter (including living plant tissue) to its mineral constituents.

GALL, an abnormal vegetative growth resulting from the feeding of usually immature insects, e.g., witches-broom in hackberry. N.B. not a burl.

GENUS (plural: genera), a group of related plants above the level of species showing similar characters and appearing to have common ancestry, e.g., the maples, cherries, and plums, dogwoods, etc.

GERMINATION, or sprouting, the development of a plantlet from a seed.

GIRDLING ROOT, a root that encircles the tree at or below the surface of the ground, interfering with flow of sap and consequently impairing the tree's health.

GLAND, properly a secreting structure on, or embedded in, the surface of a plant; also any similar protuberance such as the warty swelling at the base of the leaf in cherry and peach.

GLAUCOUS, covered with a fine waxy powder that reduces loss of water and which may be removed by heat or friction, e.g. cabbage leaf or fresh plum.

GLOMERULE, globe-shaped, dense clusters.

GRAFT, a branch or bud inserted beneath the bark of another plant with the intent that it will develop into a new plant; a scion.

GYNOECIUM, the female or pistil-bearing part of the flower.

HABIT, the general aspect of a plant, or its mode of growth.

HABITAT, the type of locality in which a plant grows.

HEAD, a dense globular inflorescence made up of many small florets; also, in reference to plant growth or habit, the top part of a plant, especially when compact.

HERBACEOUS, dying to the ground each year, the roots living over the winter; not woody.

HUMUS, decomposing organic matter in the soil.

HYBRID, a plant arising from seed produced as a result of pollination-fertilization among unlike parents; commonly the offspring of two different species.

INCISED, the margin cut sharp and deep, forming irregular teeth.

INTERNODE, the portion of stem between nodes.

KEEL, a projecting ridge on the surface, as the two front petals of a papilionaceous corolla.

KEY, a winged fruit or samara, e.g. maple, ash, tree of heaven, etc.

LARVA, the immature, wingless and often worm-like form in which certain insects hatch from the egg.

LATERAL, belonging to or borne on the side; axillary, of secondary importance.

LEADER, the primary or terminal shoot of a tree.

LEAF, the principal lateral appendage borne by the stem. *Simple* leaf when blade is not divided; *compound* leaf when it is divided into distinct parts.

LEAFLET, a single division of a compound leaf.

LEAF-STALK, the stem of a leaf; petiole.

LEGUME, pod of the pea or bean family which normally splits along both sides; also a member of that family.

LEGUMINOUS, pertaining to a legume, or to the family which is named for the legumes.

LENTICEL, lens-shaped perforation of the bark, especially on young shoots.

LOBE, a commonly rounded segment of a leaf, corolla or calyx that divides it to about the middle.

MICROCLIMATE, originally the "climate in the least space," that is in the six feet above the ground, but this concept is now expanded to include the climatic environment of very local areas, such as north-or-south-facing slopes, etc., or even smaller places, as a sheltered corner of a garden for example.

MONOECIOUS, male and female flowers separate on the same plant, as in oaks and walnuts. *See also* DIOECIOUS and COMPLETE.

MULCH, a vegetable substance, variously decomposed, or a mineral substance such as vermiculite, stone chips, etc., used on the soil around the crown of plants to condition the soil by conserving moisture, inhibiting weed growth and regulating temperature fluctuations.

NEEDLED, bearing linear, awl-shaped or scale-like leaves, as in pines, cedars, etc.

NITROGEN, colorless gas, a constituent of all living tissue.

NODE, the point on a stem at which a leaf is borne.

NODULE, a tubercle on the roots of certain leguminous plants.

OLD WOOD, more precisely the portion of a branch developed the previous year(s).

OPPOSITE, arranged in pairs; set against, as two leaves borne at a node; also as one part before another, as stamens before petals. N.B. the leaf and branch arrangement is one of the fundamental ways of identifying plants without the aid of flowers and fruits.

OVARY, that portion of the pistil containing the ovules or future seeds.

OVATE, having the outline of a hen's egg with the broadest end at the base.

OVULE, the rudimentary seed occurring in the ovary.

PANICLE, a compound, usually loose, flower cluster in which the lower branchlets are longer and blossom earlier.

PAPILIONACEOUS, referring to the flower of the Leguminosae, or pea family (also known as Papilionaceae, from the Latin, *papilio*, a butterfly).

PEDICEL, the stalk of an individual flower.

PEDUNCLE, the stalk of a flower cluster.

PETAL, a unit of the inner floral envelope, or corolla, usually colored and often showy.

229

PHOTOSYNTHESIS, the manufacture of sugar in green leaves from carbon dioxide and water by energy derived from light.

PINNATE, literally feather-formed, as leaflets on either side of a rachis.

PISTIL, the seed-bearing organ of a flower consisting of ovary, style and stigma.

POD, a splitting fruit, as a legume.

POLLARD, literally, to dehorn (hornless stag), to cut the branches back to the main stem, as practiced most often with willows and poplars.

POLLEN, the tiny grains of fertilizing "floral dust" developed within the anthers.

POLLINATION, the deposit or transfer of pollen from an anther of a flower to a stigma by means of wind, bees, etc. The pollen in due time impregnates the ovule of the flower, which results in the formation of seed. When pollen from another flower is the FERTILIZATION agent, it is called CROSS-POLLINATION. When the flower uses its own pollen, the process is called SELF-POLLINATION.

PRICKLE, a spine-like outgrowth from the bark.

PRUNING, the removal of branches from a plant in order to improve it.

RACEME, an elongated unbranched flower cluster whose rachis bears a series of single short stalked flowers, the lowermost blooming earlier.

RACHIS, an axis bearing flowers or leaflets; also spelled rhachis.

RECEPTACLE, the enlarged or elongated end of a floral axis on which the floral parts are borne.

ROOT, the underground parts of a plant that take up soluble nutrients from the soil to "feed" the top growth (and to anchor it).

230

ROSACEOUS, disposed as the five petals of a rose with stamens borne on the sepals. Also, belonging to the rose family, including cherry, plum, hawthorn.

ROSETTE, a cluster of leaves in a compact circular arrangement, so named for its resemblance to the petals of a full-blown double rose.

SAMARA, a non-splitting winged fruit, also called a key.

SCAFFOLD, the secondary branches of a tree.

SCALE (botanical), a minute leaf or bract, usually appressed and dry, serving to protect a bud before expansion; (entomological) any of numerous small but prolific homopterous insects, the young of which suck plant juices.

SCION, a slip or shoot used for grafting; also spelled cion.

SEED, the ripened ovule.

SELF-STERILE, a flower not receptive to its own pollen.

SEMI-DOUBLE, partially changed into a double flower with the inner stamens functional and the outer ones petaloid.

SEMI-EVERGREEN, retaining some of its green leaves into or throughout the winter.

SEPAL, a division of the calyx, usually green and foliaceous.

SHRUB, a woody plant, usually less than twelve feet tall and under two inches in stem diameter, which branches from the crown into several stems.

SIMPLE, undivided or unbranched.

SINGLE-FLOWERED, blooming with the normal number of petals.

SOLITARY, borne singly or alone.

SPATULATE, spoon-shaped.

SPECIES (singular and plural), a natural unit of kind among organisms; a group of individuals with so many characters in

231

common as to indicate a high degree or relationship and common descent.

SPIKE, an elongated flower cluster in which the flowers are close together and are not stalked.

SPINE, a sharp pointed rigid deep-seated emergence, differing from a thorn by its absence of vascular tissue and differing from a prickle in not pulling off with the bark.

SPUR (botanical), a hollow projection of a flower; (horticultural) a short compact branch with little or no internodal development, or with one or more internodes close together.

STAMEN, the male floral organ which bears pollen grains.

STANDARD, the upper broad petal of a papilionaceous flower.

STEM, the main axis of a plant.

STIGMA, the part of the pistil which functions to receive pollen.

STIPULES, the pair of usually leaf-like appendages borne at the base of certain leaf stalks.

STOCK, or rootstock, the plant onto which a scion is grafted.

STRATIFICATION, any process used to facilitate the germination of dormant seeds.

STRICT, said of branches which are parallel, clustered and erect.

STYLE, stalk-like often slender portion of the pistil connecting the stigma with the ovary.

TEETH, numerous small projections around the margin of a leaf (a serrate leaf).

TERMINAL, at the tip, the apical or distal end.

THORN, a hard sharp-pointed plant emergence, a woody spine, a relatively short modified branch produced from a bud, a modified stipule or a modified leaf (as on hawthorn and honeylocust; the "thorns" on a blackberry or rosebush are more properly called prickles).

232

TREE, a woody plant having usually a single well-defined stem, exceeding two inches in diameter and twelve feet in height.

TRIFOLIOLATE, said of leaves with three leaflets.

TWIG, a young woody stem; precisely, the shoot of woody plants representing the growth of the current season and terminated basally by circumferential terminal bud scars.

UMBEL, a flower cluster with flower stalks arising at the same point and of nearly equal length.

UNDERSTORY, the class of trees which form the subcanopy in a forest.

VARIETY (botanical), a subdivision of a species differing from other members in certain minor characters.

VEINS, the small ribs of the leaf framework.

WHORL, three or more leaves or flowers in a circle at a node.

WING, any membranous expansion, also (plural) the two lateral petals of a papilionaceous flower.

WOOD CHIPS, shredded branches or twigs, usually the waste from pruning operations.

Index

Accent, 3, 75, 99
Adaptability to northern gardens, 64
Aesculus carnea 'Briotii,' 85
Aesculus Hippocastanum 'Baumannii,' 85
Aesculus octandra, 86
Agricultural agent, county, 8, 149, 150, 171
Ailanthus altissima, 130, *131*
Albizia Julibrissin var. *rosea*, 118
Alder, white-, Japanese, 74, 174, 179, 182, 183, 207
Amelanchier laevis, 116, *117*
Appeal, more than one season, 10
Apples, 38, 45, 109
Application of sprays, 149
Arboretum, value of, 213
Arboretums, list of, 214-221
Arborist, 146, 148, 171
Arrangements, 11
Ash, mountain, 12, 74, 151, 177, 182, 204
   European, 75
   Korean, 74, 175, 207
Avenue trees, 70, (list) 188

Backfill, composition of, 169
Background, evergreen, 89, 97, 113, 189-192
Bark, beauty of, 22
   borer, 31
   girdled, 148
Beebee-tree, Korean, 18, 76, 175, 179, 182, 183, 207
Bees, 76, 101, 111, 128
Betula populifolia, 77, 79
Birch, gray, 19, 77, 79, 167, 174, 177, 181, 207
Birds, 2, 34, 37, 45, 72, 75, 110, 118
   migrating, 30, 40
   nesting, 137
   nuisance of, 60
   song-, effective ally of gardener, 11
   control insects, 31
   winter, 40

Blight, chestnut, 82
   fire-, 99, 109, 154
   petal, 31
Bloom, alternate year, 42
   failure to, 106, 114, 140
   forcing branches into, 209
   season of, 1
   sequence of, 194-195
Branches, forcing, 209
   pendulous, 68, 69
   spiny, 80
Buckeye, sweet, 86, 176, 178, 181
Buckthorn, woolly, 80, 174, 179, 181, 206
Budding, 163
Buds, decorative, 2
   development of, 88
   types of, 24
Bulbs, spring-blooming, 78
Bumelia lanuginosa, 80

Castanea dentata, 82
Castanea mollissima, 82
Catalpa, Chinese, 81, 175, 177, 182
Catalpa ovata, 81
Caterpillar, tent, 39, 61, 70, 152
Cedar, red, 44-46, 80, 111, 154
Cercis canadensis, 111, *112*
Cherries, 12, 15, 59, 151
Cherry, black, 72, 176, 178, 182, 183, 208
   cornelian, 14, 21, 33, *34*, 36, 174, 179, 181, 204, 208
   Fuji, 70, 174, 178, 182
   Japanese flowering, 61, 167
   Oriental (*see also* Japanese flowering), 18, 60, 174, 179, 180, 182, 183, 206, 208
   rosebud, 21, 69, 167, 175, 180
   Sargent, 69, 176, 179, 180, 208
   Yoshino, 70, 175, 178, 182, 184
Chestnut, American, 82
   Chinese, 82, *83*, 175, 178, 181, 184, 208
   horse, double, 84, 176, 178, 182
   ruby, 85, 176, 178, 180
   trees, 18, 21, *83*

235

INDEX

Chestnuts, 14
Chickadees, 78
Chionanthus retusus, 93
Chionanthus virginicus, 93
Choosing flowering trees, 5-9
Cladrastis lutea, 139
Clethra barbinervis, 74
Climate control, 3
  micro-, 147
Cold temperature for treating seeds, 158
Color, flower, 180-183
  foliage, autumn, 19
  in landscape, 17
Commission, shade tree, 193
Competition among plants, 150
Composition in garden for special season, 7
  in landscape, 17
  of soil, 142
Conifer background, 47, 189-190
Cornus controversa, 36
  coreana, 33
  florida, 28, 29
    'Pendula,' 31
    'Pluribracteata,' 31
    var. *rubra,* 31
    'Welchii,' 31
  Kousa, 32
  mas, 33, 34
  Nuttallii, 32
  officinalis, 36
Cotinus Coggygria, 122, *123*
Crabapple, American, 44
  Arnold, 41, 174, 178, 182, 184, 205
  Bechtel, 176, 178, 180, 184
  carmine, 47, 174, 179, 180, 184, 204, 205
  cutleaf, 46, 176, 177, 182, 184, 204, 208
  Dorothea, 43, 174, 179, 180, 184, 205
  flowering, Chinese, 42, 176, 178, 182, 184
  Japanese, 40, 174, 179, 182, 184, 205
  Katherine, 43, 174, 179, 182, 184, 205
  Lemoine, 47, 174, 179, 181, 184, 205
  Parkman, 44, 174, 178, 180, 184, 205
  Sargent, 46, 174, 179, 182, 184, 205
  Scheidecker, 41, 174, 179, 180, 184, 205

  slender Siberian, 45, 176, 178, 182, 184, 204
  tea, 41, 174, 179, 182, 184, 205
Crabapples, 14, 15, 38, 46, 151, 167
Crataegus Phaenopyrum, 97
Critical periods of reflected heat, 147
Cuttings, 161

Damage, winter, 19
Davidia involucrata, 86
Diseases, 149
  rosaceous, 154
Distance, planting, 29
Dogwood, Chinese, 21, 32
  flowering, 23, *28,* 29, 167
  giant, 12, 21, 36
  Korean, 24, 33
  Pacific, 32
  pagoda, 36
Dogwoods, 27, 174, 179, 182, 204, 203
Dormancy of seeds, 158
Dormant oil spray *(see* Spray)
Dove-tree, 18, 86, 177, 182
Drought, 30, 82, 85, 134, 143, 146
  tree insensitive to, 80, 132

Effect, floral, fountainlike, 46
Effects of drought, 142
Ehretia, heliotrope, 87, 174, 177, 183, 184, 208
Ehretia thyrsiflora, 87
Elaeagnus angustifolia, 106
Empress-tree, *13,* 18, *25,* 88, 178, 181
Enemies, insect, battle with, 11
Epaulette-tree, 89, *90, 91,* 176, 177, 183
Establishment, plant, 64
Evergreen, needled, 32, 127
  tree, 87
Evergreens, 113, 128
Evodia Daniellii, 76

Fertilizer application, 143
Filler among tall trees, 3
Flowering, alternate year, 42
Flowers, double, 31, 42, 43, 44, 59, 60, 63, 84
  semi-double, 67

single, 59, 63
wild, 118
Foliage, autumn colored, 19, 70, 207-208
  blue-green, 17
  bold mass effects of, 18
  evergreen, contrast with, 43
  fine, 17
  other than green, 71
  red, effect of, 17
  season, length of, 2
Forcing branches for flower shows, 209
Form, tree, basic types of, 21
  classes of, 177-180
Fragrance, 183-185
  emphasizing, 14
  season, 17
Franklin-tree, 92, 167, 175, 177, 183, 208
Franklinia alatamaha, 92
Fringe-trees, 19, 93, 175, 178, 183, 205, 207
Fruit, 11
Fruits as table delicacies, 2
  attractive to birds, 2
  dessert, 14
  dried, 14
  fleshy, 11, (list) 204-206
  second season of attraction, 11
Fumigant, anti-borer, 31
Fungicide, 31
Fungus, cedar-apple rust, 44, 46, 99, 154

Garden, enclosed, 7
  intimate, 101
  picture, 3
  -serviceman, a specialist, 145
Gardens, botanical, 213
  neighborhood, 4
  public, 213
  suburban, 145
Germination, 157
Golden-chain, Waterer's, 94, 175, 179, 181
Goldenrain-tree, 18, 95, *96,* 176, 178, 181, 207
Grafting, bridge, 148
  purpose of, 162
Green of foliage, 113
Group (grove) of trees, 188-190

Guy wires, 193

Halesia carolina, 119, *120, 121*
Halesia monticola, 119
  'Rosea,' 122
Haw, black, 21, 23, *138,* 175, 178, 183, 184, 204, 206, 208
Hawthorn, English, 97, *98*
  Washington, 97, 175, 178, 183, 184, 204, 208
Hawthorns, 151, 167
Heat reflection, 147
Height classes of flowering trees, 174-177
Hemlock, 128, 189
Herbicides, 150
Hole dimensions, 169
Home, modern, planting about, 52
  property, can accommodate flowering trees, 4
Hovenia dulcis, 110

Identification table based on flowers, 196-203
Idesia, 16, 18, 176, 178, 181, 204
Idesia polycarpa, 99
Inarching, 148
Injury to plants, common causes of, 141
Insecticide, risk of handling, 149
Insects, boring, twig-, 105
  control of, 144, 149
  effects of, 146, 149
  mining, leaf-, 105
  scale, 153
Interplanting among shade trees, 78
Interval, planting (*see also* Planting distance), 33, 82
Irrigation, 64, 170

Jelly, 14, 34

Koelreuteria paniculata, 95, *96*

Label directions, spray, 144
Labeled tree collections (*see also* Arboretum list), 4
Laburnum Watereri, 94

INDEX

Landscape anchor, 3
  designer, 186
  maintenance man, 171
Lawn, 114, 118
Layering, 163
Leaf-miner, birch, 79
  locust, 105
Leaves, compound, 17
Light, reflected, 147
Lightening, 148
Lilac, Peking, 100, 178, 181, 184
  tree, Japanese, 100, 175, 177, 181, 184
Limes, 103
Limestone, 113
Lindens, 16, 101, *102*, 103, 176, 177, 178, 181, 184
Liriodendron Tulipifera, 134, *135*
Locust, black, 16, 18, 104, 177, 178, 183, 184

Maackia, 106, 180, 181, 184
Maackia amurensis, 106
Magnolia, anise, 56, 176, 177, 183
Magnolia denudata, 52
Magnolia, evergreen, 57, 176, 177, 183, 184
Magnolia grandiflora, 57
Magnolia Kobus, 52, *53*, 176, 177, 183, 184
  var. *stellata*, *50*, *51*, 52
Magnolia liliflora, 56
Magnolia, rustica, 180
Magnolia salicifolia, 56
Magnolia, saucer, 21, 53, *54*, 175, 179, 184
Magnolia Soulangiana, 53, *54*
  'Lennei,' 53, *55*
Magnolia, star, *50*, *51*, 52
Magnolia, sweetbay, 24, 57, 175, 180, 185, 207
Magnolia virginiana, 57
Magnolia, yulan, 52, 176, 179, 183, 185
Magnolias, 15, 23, 48, 167, 204, 205
Malus arnoldiana, 41
  atrosanguinea, 47
  baccata 'Gracilis,' 45
  coronaria 'Charlottae,' 44
  'Dorothea,' 43
  floribunda, 40

Halliana 'Parkmanii,' 44
hupehensis, 41
ioensis 'Prince Georges,' 44
  'Katherine,' 43
  purpurea 'Lemoinei,' 47
  'Red Jade,' 46
Sargentii, 46
Scheideckeri, 41
spectabilis 'Riversii,' 42
toringoides, 46
Mice, 30, 152
Moisture, conserving, 143
  soil, 30
Mulch, 64, 118, 127, 152, 170
  soil, 107
  woodchip, 30, 143

Newspaper bulletins, 149
Nursery catalogues, 4
Nutrients, mineral, 141
  needing yearly replacement, 143
  plant, for growth, 143

Oleaster, 106
Olive, Russian-, 12, 16, 18, 106, 175, 179, 181, 185, 205
Organic matter, 146
Oxydendrum arboreum, 127

Park trees, 193
Paulownia tomentosa, *13*, 25, 88
Peach, flowering, 14, 64, 151, 175, 180, 181, 183, 185
Pear, Callery, 107, *108*, 151, 176, 178, 183, 185, 205, 208
Photinia, 151, 175, 180, 183, 204, 208
Photinia villosa, 12, 110
Pine, 189
  lacebark, 130
  white, 128
Plan tree planting, 7, 169
Planting, careful, 147
  labeled, 213
  too deeply, effect of, 150
Plum, beach, 71, 175, 179, 183, 185, 204, 205, 208
  purple-leaved, 71, 175, 179, 181

Plums, 12, 14
Poison-ivy, 150
Poisoned bait, 152
Pollution, atmospheric, tree indifference to, 132
Practices, pruning, basic, 171-172
Problems, possible, 141
Productive tree on poor sites, 132
Propagation, 155-164
Pruning, 99, 105
  for flower production, 172
  infected branches, 154
  magnolias, 57
  maintenance, 171
  to compensate for root loss, 145
Prunus cerasifera 'Pissardii,' 71
Prunus 'Hally Jolivette,' 69
  incisa, 70
  maritima, 71
  Sargentii, 69
  serotina, 72
  serrulata, 61
    'Amanogawa,' 66
    'Fugenzo,' 65
    "James Veitch," 66
    'Jo-nioi,' 68
    'Kwanzan,' 65
    'Oshima-zakura,' 67
    'Shirofugen,' 66
    'Shogetsu,' 65
    'Sirotae,' 66
    'Taihaku-zakura,' 67
    'Tanabata,' 67
  subhirtella, 68
    'Beni-higan,' 69
    'Jagatsu-zakura,' 68
    'Shidare-higan,' 69
  yedoensis, 70
Pterostyrax hispida, 89, *90*, *91*
Pyrus Calleryana, 107, *108*
  'Bradford,' 108

Quality, criterion of, 8
  of nursery stock, 9

Rabbit injury to bark, 52
Radiation, excessive, effects of, 147

Raisin-tree, 110, 176, 177, 182, 205
Redbud, 111, *112*, 167, 175, 179, 181, 207
Reflected light and heat, 147
Requirements, cultural, 5
  water, 142
Robinia Pseudoacacia, 104
Robins, 30, 118
Rodent repellant, 148
Root loss compensated by pruning, 145
  system, balled and burlaped, 152
Roots burned by fertilizer application, 144
  girdling, 146
  of plants for sale, 8
  seedling, advantages of, 155
  unwind, of container grown plants, 147
Rose family notes, 151
Rules for watering, 142

Sanitation to combat diseases, 149, 154
Sawdust of bark-borer, 31
Scale insects, 153
  tulip, 58
Scholar-tree, 18, 19, 24, 114, *115*, 167, 177, 181, 205, 207
Screen, 81, 87, 99
  wind, 107
Seashore gardens, 18, 106
Season for transplanting, 167
Seed bed, preparation of, 157
Seed cases, 11
  coats, impervious, 158
  cleaning, 156
  collecting, 156
  coming true from, 42
  handling, 157
  signs of ripeness, 156
  testing of, 156
Seeds, 155
  handling, 157
  instructions for planting, 157
  testing for viability, 156
Seedling care, 160
  root system, 155
Selecting flowering trees for year round interest, 10
Service-berry, 12, 23, 116, *117*, 175, 178, 183, 205, 208

INDEX

Setting, 6
Sexes on separate trees, 99, 133
Shad-blow, 151
Shade, dense, 82, 83
  tree commission, 193
Shelter, 87
Sheltered spot, survival in, 124
Show, flower, 209
Sign of thorough spray coverage, 153
Signs to buy by, 8
Silk-tree, hardy, 118, 175, 180, 181, 185
Silverbells, 119, *120*, *121*, 175, 176, 179,
  181, 183, 207
Size of hole for transplanting, 169
  tree, 9
Skill in transplanting, 169
Smoke-tree, 12, 122, *123*, 175, 179, 182,
  205, 208
Snowbells, 16, 21, 125, *126*, 127, 167, 176,
  177, 183, 185
Soil, acid, 127
  alkaline, 95
  compaction, 145
  composition, 142
  potting, 157
  pulverizing, 145
  soak the, 143
  structure, disturbed, 145
Sophora japonica, 114, *115*
Sorbus alnifolia, 74
Sorbus Aucuparia, 75
Sourwood, 23, 127, 167, 176, 178, 182, 208
Specimen tree, free-standing, 37, 41, 99,
  186-187
  lawn, 40
Spray, dormant oil, 39, 58, 153
Spraying to control insects, 80
  preventive, 99
Sprays, chemical, caution in handling, 149
  for pest control, 144, 149
  old-fashioned, 149
Squirrels, 2, 12
Stabilization of sandy soils and steep
  banks, 105
Staking tree trunk, 170
Stewartia koreana, 128
  ovata var. *grandiflora*, *129*, 130

Pseudo-Camellia, 130
Stewartias, 128, *129*, 130, 176, 178, 183,
  208
Street tree, 114
  criteria, 193
Styrax japonica, 125, *126*
Styrax Obassia, 127
Suburban garden, 145
Succession of bloom, 7, (chart) 194-195
Syringa japonica var. *amurensis*, 100
Syringa pekinensis, 100

Terms, tree, to know, 222-233
  of sale and replacement, 8
Thorns, 105, 109
Tilia cordata, 103
Tilia euchlora, 103
Tilia petiolaris, 103
Tilia platyphylla, 101
Tilia tomentosa, 103
Tolerances, cultural, 5
Trained plant to single stem, 93, 136-137
Traits, tree, 174-208
Transplanted trees, recent, 145
Transplanting, balled and burlaped (B &
  B), 168
  hints, 165
  fall *versus* spring, 167
Tree of heaven, 105, 130, *131*, 177, 179,
  182, 207
Trees, languishing, 150
Trunk guard, 148
Tulip-tree, 19, 20, 134, *135*, 167, 177, 182,
  207
Turf, 37, 68, 82, 104
Twig, beauty of, 22

Uses, special, of trees, 186-193

Viburnum prunifolium, 136, 138
Viburnum, Siebold, 12, 18, 137, 176, 179,
  183, 185, 206
Viburnum Sieboldii, 137
Vines, 150

Water requirements, 161, 170
  table, 146

240

Watering (*see also* Irrigation), 142
Waxwings, cedar, 30
Webworm, mimosa, 119
Weeds, 150

Wisteria, 94

Yellowwood, 16, 18, 22, 23, 139, 176, 180, 183, 185, 207